THE LAND
OF THE
CLIFF-DWELLERS

Frederick H. Chapin

THE LAND
OF THE
CLIFF-DWELLERS

Foreword by Robert H. Lister

THE UNIVERSITY OF ARIZONA PRESS
TUCSON

THE UNIVERSITY OF ARIZONA PRESS

Copyright © 1988
The Arizona Board of Regents
All Rights Reserved

93   92   91   90   89   88

5   4   3   2   1

Manufactured in the U.S.A.

Library of Congress Cataloging-in-Publication Data

Chapin, Frederick H. (Frederick Hastings)
    The land of the cliff-dwellers / Frederick H. Hastings; foreword
by Robert H. Lister.
        p.   cm.
    Reprint. Originally published: Boston: Appalachian Mountain Club,
1892. With new foreword.
    Bibliography: p.
    Includes index.
    ISBN 0-8165-1052-0 (alk. paper)
    1. Southwest, New — Description and travel.   2. Indians of North
America — Southwest, New.   3. Cliff-dwellings — Southwest, New.
4. Pueblo Indians.   5. Mesa Verde National Park (Colo.)   6. Chapin,
Frederick H. (Frederick Hastings)   I. Title
F786.C46 1988
979'.00497 — dc19   87-30253
                                                                         CIP

British Library Cataloguing in Publication data are available.

C O N T E N T S.

FOREWORD.

ROBERT H. LISTER

THE best known and most frequently visited cliff dwellings of Mesa Verde National Park—including the largest, Cliff Palace, and other well-known ruins such as Spruce Tree House, Balcony House, Oak Tree House, and Square Tower House — are located in natural alcoves along the cliffs of Chapin Mesa. On the relatively flat surface of the same piñon pine – juniper – oak – clad mesa, there are the ruins of Far View House, Sun Temple, Mummy Lake, and the excavated pithouses and small pueblos situated along the Ruins Road loop. The National Park Service visitor center, archaeological museum, headquarters installation, staff residences, and utility areas, and the Far View Lodge complex are also situated on Chapin Mesa.

This archaeologically important and highly utilized section of Mesa Verde National Park is named for Frederick Hastings Chapin, who visited the region during the summers of 1889 and 1890. He described the landscape and its then

known antiquities in an 1890 article, "Cliff-dwellings of the Mancos Cañons," and subsequently in
the book, *The Land of the Cliff-Dwellers*, published in 1892.

Gustaf Nordenskiöld, credited with conducting
and reporting upon the first systematic explorations in the cliff dwellings of Mesa Verde, desig-
nated the mesa, "bounded to the east by Cliff
Cañon [now called Soda Canyon], to the west by a
fork of Navajo Cañon, and indented at the sides by
numerous small cañons . . . *Chapin's Mesa* after
F. H. Chapin, who was the first to publish any description of some of the more important ruins of
the Mesa Verde" (Nordenskiöld, 1893, pp. 49–
50). Through time the name has been shortened
to Chapin Mesa. Nordenskiöld, whose investigations in and about Mesa Verde took place during
the fall of 1891, knew of Chapin's earlier activities there through the article Chapin published in
1890.

Frederick H. Chapin's visits to Mesa Verde were
an outgrowth of his avid interest in mountains
and mountaineering, particularly in respect to the
Rocky Mountains of Colorado, which by 1889 had
resulted in a series of articles describing his experiences among those slopes and his first book,
*Mountaineering in Colorado: The Peaks about
Estes Park.*

Luther and Angelina Chapin lived in Lafayette, Indiana, a thriving community on the banks of the Wabash River, where Luther was a merchant. Their first child, Frederick Hastings, was born on September 5, 1852. In 1856 the Chapins moved to the uproarious frontier community of Leavenworth, Kansas. Luther found employment as a salesman in that bustling town, which served as eastern terminus for both the Oregon and Santa Fe trails and was home of Fort Leavenworth, the military supply depot for the government's western outposts. About that time, a second child, Gertrude Eliza, was born to the Chapins. In 1862 Angelina died, and Luther was left to raise his ten-year-old son and six-year-old daughter.

In Leavenworth, young Frederick led a busy, adventuresome life, which apparently fostered his later interests in travel and outdoor activities. He mingled with soldiers at the barracks, visited Indians on nearby reservations, and rode horseback for miles on the prairies, accompanying wagon trains for a distance as they slowly began their long winding treks westward.

Although Luther Chapin remarried, both Frederick and Gertrude were sent east to the home of their aunt, Mrs. Thomas Sisson, in Hartford, Connecticut, in 1864. Mr. Sisson was a leading Hartford citizen and head of Sisson and Butler, a respected and prosperous wholesale and retail drug firm. The Sissons lived in affluent West Hartford with their two daughters. The Chapin children were raised as members of their own family.

For Frederick, life in the stability of the Sisson household and in cosmopolitan, conservative Hartford was a great change from the rambunctious lifestyle of bustling Leavenworth. He attended the local district school for a year and high school for another year. Then, at age 15 he entered his uncle's drug business. He did not seem to have had any additional formal academic training, but became well-educated through his own efforts. He read widely, especially in literature dealing with travel and exploration, developed an ability to write properly and with clarity, and cultivated poise and self-confidence that permitted him to move comfortably in the social and business circles of the Sissons and their associates.

Frederick prospered in the drug business. At age 29 he was advanced to partnership in Sisson, Chandler, and Chapin, as the firm was renamed. This role provided Chapin the financial means and leisure time to pursue more actively his long-time interests in travel and exploration.

Actually, his enthusiasm for mountaineering began earlier but was limited to climbing in the adjacent Connecticut hills, Adirondacks, and White Mountains. In 1877, he and several of his New England friends, among them Charles P. Howard, who later was to accompany Frederick on many of his Colorado adventures, spent part of the summer in Switzerland climbing in the Alps. Membership in the Appalachian Mountain Club, to which he was admitted about 1880, stimulated Chapin's outdoor interests and provided him a forum for exchanging accounts of mountaineering adventures and meeting others with similar avocations and the opportunity to participate in organized excursions, as well as furnishing a mechanism for publishing narratives of some of his experiences.

The Appalachian Mountain Club was founded in Boston in 1876 to further exploration of the mountains of New England and vicinity, both for scientific and artistic purposes and to cultivate a general interest in geography. Its quarterly journal, *Appalachia*, featured articles by club members. Chapin sometimes traveled to Boston to attend the club's meetings. He personally presented several papers to the membership, but on other occasions, when he was unable to attend meetings, he had friends read his papers. Seven of his mountaineering accounts were published in *Appalachia*.

In 1882, Chapin married Alice Louise Seavey

of West Hartford. They honeymooned in Switzerland, where Frederick for the second time climbed some of the Alpine peaks. Thereafter, his vacation-related mountaineering activities shifted to the Rocky Mountains of Colorado.

It is evident that Chapin made at least four trips to Estes Park and other mountainous regions of Colorado between the years 1886 and 1889, and there is reason to believe that possibly as many as eight separate trips were made to Colorado. He drew together accounts of several of his Colorado experiences and published them in a single volume in 1889. *Mountaineering in Colorado: The Peaks about Estes Park* was published under the auspices of the Appalachian Mountain Club, which advanced $350 to partially cover printing costs. The book was profusely illustrated with photographs taken by Chapin, who used the cumbersome view camera, tripod, and fragile glass plates that were part of the dry plate photographic process of that day. An appendix listing the flora of Estes Park was based on collections made by his wife, Alice. The book was well received and was reprinted in several editions, both in the United States and in Great Britain. In 1987 it was reprinted by the University of Nebraska Press. In that volume, the original edition has been enhanced and updated by a foreword and notes authored by James H. Pickering.

Chapin's last two vacations in Colorado, in 1889 and 1890, took him to the San Juan Mountains in the southwestern corner of the state, where he not only rambled among the high Rockies but also investigated the newly discovered Indian antiquities of the Mesa Verde. Upon returning to Hartford after his first visit to Mesa Verde, he prepared an illustrated paper, "Cliff-dwellings of the Mancos Cañons," which he delivered to his Appalachian Mountain Club colleagues. It was judged so significant that publication soon followed in both the May 1890 number of *Appalachia* and in volume 12 (1890) of the *American Antiquarian and Oriental Journal*.

After his second summer at Mesa Verde, Chapin consolidated his notes on the cliff dwellings and the San Juans, researched the native peoples and Spanish exploration and occupation of the Southwest, and reviewed previous investigations around Mesa Verde. He put them together in his second book, *The Land of the Cliff-Dwellers*, published in 1892 in Boston by the Appalachian Mountain Club.

Alice Chapin died the year before Frederick began his Mesa Verde adventures. He remained a widower until 1898, when he married a second cousin, Mary Hastings Potter of Lafayette, Indiana. The couple resided in Hartford, but fourteen months following the marriage, after a prolonged illness, Frederick H. Chapin died of tuberculosis on January 25, 1900.

The final eight years of Chapin's life are not well documented. For example, it cannot be verified that he visited India in 1894 to climb in the Himalayas, although it has been so stated. It is known that before he remarried he built an elegant mountain lodge-like house for himself in West Hartford. It featured a wood interior, had a two-story beamed living room with massive stone fireplace, and simple masculine furnishings.

It is not known how Chapin learned of the Indian ruins of the Mesa Verde region nor why he chose to spend parts of two summers examining them. Whether his concern with archaeology stemmed from his Mesa Verde experiences or whether he traveled to Mesa Verde because of a prior interest in antiquities also is not clear. Perhaps his youthful association with Indians around Leavenworth, Kansas, instigated a lifelong concern for Native Americans present and past.

Chapin was a member of the Hartford Archaeological Society in 1890. In a letter dated April 7, 1890, in which Richard Wetherill sought to interest Professor Frederic W. Putnam, director of the Peabody Museum, Harvard University, in the cliff dwellings of Mesa Verde, Richard wrote, "Through the kindness of Frederick H. Chapin, of the Hartford Archaeological Society, I received your address . . . " (McNitt, 1966, p. 329). Is it possible that Frederick may have become an archaeological society member and have met Professor Putnam only after his 1889 visit to Mesa Verde, while he was researching his paper on the cliff dwellings of Mancos Canyon?

By the time Chapin first journeyed to Mesa Verde in 1889, most of the major cliff dwellings, including such grand structures as Cliff Palace, Balcony House, and Spruce Tree House, situated in the fingerlike canyons of the Mesa Verde uplift and in Mancos Canyon to the south, had been discovered. Many of them had been dug over by local residents searching for "relics." The Wetherill family of Mancos, Colorado, took the lead in locating ruins and in collecting quantities of materials left in them by their last inhabitants, now called the Anasazi and known to be ancestral to modern Pueblo Indians.

As Chapin relates in this volume, he fortuitously found his way to Benjamin Kite Wetherill's Alamo Ranch on the banks of the Mancos River just west of the flat-topped, green-clad plateau that may have been named Mesa Verde by eighteenth-century Spanish explorers. The Wetherill family had homesteaded the land in

1881. As they developed their ranch lands, the many mounds of tumbled building stones littered with broken pottery and other artifacts that marked the ruins of former Indian habitations attracted their attention. More significantly, while running cattle on the Mesa Verde they came across well-preserved cliff dwellings clinging to the walls of the mesa's canyons. This stimulated such interest on the part of the Wetherill brothers that, beginning in the mid-1880s, they devoted a great deal of time and energy to locating additional cliff dwellings and searching for artifacts in them.

At the Alamo Ranch Chapin was told of the profusion of cliff dwellings and other archaeological features strewn about the valleys, cliffs, and mesas of the region, and was shown many examples of specimens recovered from them. Desiring to see and photograph these "symbols of the past," as the Wetherills came to regard the cliff dwellings (Wetherill, 1977, p. 104), Chapin solicited their aid in getting into the rough country. The cliff dwellings were located over routes known only to the Wetherills and a few others. During Chapin's two visits to the cliff-house country, the three oldest Wetherill brothers — Richard, Al, and John — served at various times as his outfitters and guides. Apparently Chapin did no digging, being content to draw sketches and take notes and photographs of the cliff dwellings and their natural settings and to photograph specimens the Wetherills had collected.

Chapin was one of the first to be guided to the cliff dwellings after the Wetherills had explored the entire region, mapped it, and named most of the canyons and ruins. Thereafter, the Wetherills catered to the tourist trade, devoting as much or more time to that endeavor as they did to farming and raising cattle. Between 1889 and 1901, Al Wetherill estimated that nearly 1,000 "ordinary sight-seers, teachers, scientific men, and world travelers visited the ranch to see the cliff dwellings" (Wetherill, 1977, pp. 179–181). A popular three-day trip that included Cliff Palace, Spruce Tree House, and Square Tower House, cost $20 per person. Some of their clients became life-long associates and friends. Others were put out of mind as quickly as possible, such as one woman tourist who insisted upon taking a portable canvas bathtub on an extended seventeen-day trip.

After his first experience at Mesa Verde, Chapin promptly prepared his paper on the cliff dwellings for delivery to the Appalachian Mountain Club, and probably also to the Hartford Archaeological Society. It was published in 1890. *The Land of the Cliff-Dwellers* was written and printed after the second excursion to Mesa Verde in 1890. It incorporated data and photographs from both trips and appeared in 1892. Although the volume did not claim to be a scientific treatise, it was felt that the archaeological community would welcome its accurate description of the vestiges of an ancient Pueblo culture.

However, Chapin's efforts were to be eclipsed by those of Gustaf Nordenskiöld, a young Swedish scientist and traveler, who came to the Mesa Verde area in 1891. He, too, engaged the services of the Wetherill brothers to lead him to the ruins and to help him explore them in a more scientific manner than had Chapin. He compiled a record of detailed notes and photographs, and acquired a large collection of artifacts, which resulted in a second book on the archaeology of the remote region less than a decade after the discovery of Cliff Palace.

Nordenskiöld's book, *The Cliff Dwellings of the Mesa Verde, Southwestern Colorado: Their Pottery and Implements*, was published in Swedish in 1893, followed shortly by an English translation. It received wider attention at the time than Chapin's, and today is considered a landmark in the pioneer scientific studies of the Southwest (Arrhenius, 1986; Brew, 1946, p. 21; Willey and Sabloff, 1974, p. 59).

Despite Nordenskiöld's greater public recognition, it was he who named the largest tableland of the Mesa Verde complex Chapin's Mesa in honor of his predecessor. Moreover, today Chapin is credited with publishing the earliest widely distributed information on the archaeology of the Mesa Verde region (Breternitz, 1983, p. 225). His descriptive ability and photographic competence, whetted by his many mountaineering accounts, are evident in the following narrative, as is his aptitude to review, digest, and synthesize historical and anthropological literature. These are fields that he touched upon only slightly in other writings.

To be sure, Frederick H. Chapin carried his avocations well beyond those of most of his colleagues, both physically and mentally. In delivering lectures and publishing articles and books about his adventures, he contributed to the enjoyment and knowledge of many. The following discourse still fulfills those objectives.

NOTES AND REFERENCES.

Notes

The following notes correlate some of Chapin's terms and names or descriptions of ruins and geographical features with those currently in use so that the reader may equate parts of the narrative with modern nomenclature.

Identification of Unnamed Cliff Dwellings in Text
Page 130 and following: Probably refers to Eagle Nest House, named by Earl H. Morris in 1913. Morris gained access to the

cliff dwelling by using the two poles
placed against the cliff below the
site by the Wetherills.
Page 147 and following: Cliff dwelling is Spruce Tree
House.
Pages 151 and 152: Cliff dwelling is Step House.
Page 152 and following: Cliff dwelling is Long House.

Acknowledgments
Details of Frederick H. Chapin's life have been abstracted
from James H. Pickering's excellent Foreword and Notes to
the 1987 reprint of *Mountaineering in Colorado: The
Peaks about Estes Park.* Assistance in researching Chapin's life was also gratefully received from Jack E. Smith,
Mesa Verde National Park; Mrs. Howard R. Chapin, Dyer, Indiana; and Mrs. Patricia Potter Duncan, Palo Alto, California.

References

Arrhenius, O. W.
    1986. *Stones Speak and Waters Sing: The Life and
          Works of Gustaf Nordenskiöld.* Edited and an-
          notated by Robert H. and Florence C. Lister.
          Mesa Verde Museum Association, Mesa Verde
          National Park, Colorado.
Breternitz, D.A.
    1983. Mesa Verde National Park: A History of its Ar-
          chaeology. *Essays and Monographs in Col-
          orado History,* no. 2, p. 225, Colorado Historical
          Society, Denver.
Brew, J. O.
    1946. Archaeology of Alkali Ridge, Southeastern Utah.
          *Papers of the Peabody Museum of American
          Archaeology and Ethnology,* vol. 21, Cam-
          bridge, Massachusetts.

Chapin, F. H.
  1889. *Mountaineering in Colorado: The Peaks about Estes Park.* Appalachian Mountain Club, Boston. (Reprinted in 1987, with foreword and notes by James H. Pickering, by the University of Nebraska Press, Lincoln.)
  1890. Cliff-dwellings of the Mancos Cañons. *American Antiquarian and Oriental Journal*, vol. 12, no. 4, p. 193; and *Appalachia*, vol. 6 (May 1890), p. 12.
  1892. *The Land of the Cliff-Dwellers.* Appalachian Mountain Club, W. B. Clarke and Co., Boston.

Holmes, W. H.
  1878. Report on the Ancient Ruins of Southwestern Colorado, Examined during the Summers of 1875 and 1876. *United States Geological and Geographical Survey of the Territories for 1876, 10th Annual Report*, p. 383, Washington, D. C.

McNitt, F.
  1966. *Richard Wetherill: Anasazi.* University of New Mexico Press, Albuquerque.

Morris, E. H.
  1919. Preliminary Account of the Antiquities of the Region between the Mancos and LaPlata Rivers in Southwestern Colorado. *Bureau of American Ethnology, 33rd Annual Report*, p. 155, Washington, D. C.

Nordenskiöld, G.
  1893. *The Cliff Dwellers of the Mesa Verde, Southwestern Colorado: Their Pottery and Implements.* Translated by D. Lloyd Morgan. P. A. Norstedt and Soner, Stockholm and Chicago. (Reprinted in 1979 by the Rio Grande Press, Glorieta, New Mexico.)

Wetherill, B. A.

    1977. *The Wetherills of the Mesa Verde. Autobiography of Benjamin Alfred Wetherill.* Edited and annotated by Maurine S. Fletcher. Associated University Press, Cranberry, New Jersey and London.

Willey, G. R., and J. A. Sabloff

    1974. *A History of American Archaeology.* W. H. Freeman and Co., San Francisco.

P R E F A C E.

FOR a number of years I have passed my vacations in rambling in the high Rockies, and as a variation from mountain-climbing have spent some time investigating the antiquities of Colorado. It is a description of ruins and relics which occupies an important part of this work, though the mountains have not been neglected.

With few exceptions, the pictures are copies from my own negatives.* For four very interesting views of pueblos I am indebted to the Bureau of Ethnology, and for a view in Socorro, and of a ruined adobe church, to Dr. F. M. Endlich, of Colorado. The reproductions were made by the Art Publishing Company of Boston. The general maps are based upon Government publications, the details of which I have filled in from various authorities. The map of the Mesa Verde is based upon that published in Hayden's Reports, and upon the beautiful panoramic views of Mr. William H. Holmes. I have added a number of cañons not placed upon the original map, and have located a number of ruins. The map has been redrawn by Mr. J. J. Nairn in a manner to show the plateaus and cañons in relief.

*All photographs and most maps have been omitted from the 1987 edition.

Though I have had occasion to quote from the work of Ternaux-Compans, the repository for the published documents of the early Spanish explorers, in the main I have preferred to follow the accounts given in the recent works of A. F. Bandelier, H. H. Bancroft, and the "Narrative and Critical History of America," edited by Justin Winsor, for the reason that these writers have had the advantage of consulting copies of manuscripts and other printed documents, and have been able to correct errors in the French translations. I am under especial obligations to the works of A. F. Bandelier. This well-known authority, under the auspices of the Archaeological Institute of America, has investigated the ruins of the Southwest and made a study of the existing tribes. Well equipped with the knowledge of the Spanish historical documents, he has been able to give us a clear picture of explorations as related by the early chroniclers. His works are published in the papers of the Archaeological Institute of America, American Series, of which Parts I., II., III., and V. have been issued. Of the works of Hubert Howe Bancroft — likewise gratefully acknowledged as the source of much valuable information — the volumes principally consulted are vols. i.–v., "Native Races;" vols. xiv., xv., "The North Mexican States;" vol. xvii., "Arizona and New Mexico;" vol. xxv., "Nevada, Colorado, and Wyoming;" and vols. xxvii. and xxviii.

The text that follows is a direct photographic reproduction of the 1892 edition published by W. B. Clarke and Company, Boston, with original pagination retained.

CAÑONS
OF THE
MANCOS RIVER.
COLORADO.

37° N. LAT.

IMPORTANT CLIFF HOUSES
LOWLAND AND MESA RUINS

THE

LAND OF THE CLIFF-DWELLERS.

———◆———

CHAPTER I.

THE LAND OF THE CLIFF-DWELLERS.

BEYOND the southern Rockies, where Utah, Arizona, and New Mexico border upon Colorado's frontier lines, is a strange land, inhabited by strange people, and containing monuments and relics of yet stranger tribes of an unknown antiquity.

From the melting snows of lofty sierras, rivers far larger than those of the present day once ran to the south and west, cutting out in the sandstone plateau a network of cañons that gives to the landscape an appearance resembling the face of the moon. Among some of these deep cuts and weird valleys dwell remnants of wild tribes which once hunted among the mountains to the

north and east. All along the banks of the San
Juan River and some of its tributaries are gathered
bands of the Ute Indians, who, in more remote districts, far from the agencies of the reservation, still
live a primitive life. Over the Colorado line in
Arizona is the reservation of the Navajos, and to
the south and west of these are the pueblos of
the Zuñis, Moquis, and other tribes. These latter
live in communistic towns built of stone and
adobe, and some of them, at least, are supposed
to be the descendants of the prehistoric race, —
a once great people, the ruins of whose edifices
are found here upon cliff and in valley throughout a broad zone. In fact, this field of ruins
extends from the Sierra Nevada range on the
west to Texas on the east, the existing pueblo
towns occupying but a small portion of this great
territory. These, as well as the ruins of similar
recently abandoned adobe and rubble buildings
in the valleys and on the mesas, are very interesting; yet remains of cliff-dwellings among the
cañons are the prehistoric factors which are by
far more fascinating.[1]

[1] In using the term "prehistoric" in these pages, I am not
implying any great age to the relics and ruins, but maintain
that they antedate the coming of the Spaniards, that there
are no written records in regard to them, and that traditions
are very meagre.

Imagine a lone traveller, having crossed the great Continental Divide, pursuing his way westward over the lofty plain. At his back are the mighty crests of the San Juan Mountains. Rising here and there from the dreary level are strange, weird volcanic rocks, alone relieving the seemingly endless area of desert. As he crosses feeble watercourses, rivulets that are making their way toward the great Colorado River to mingle at last with the gentle surf of the Pacific, he may see an occasional ranch, with horses or cattle feeding near the water. On drier pasture he may find sheep feeding on the scant herbage, guarded by Navajo herders. These, and perhaps a jack-rabbit or a prairie-dog colony, are all that he will see to relieve the treeless country and the awful stillness and parchedness of the sage-brush plain. If he is ignorant of the existence of the former populations, our traveller may imagine for the moment that this land has always been given over to the antelope, the coyote, the prairie-dog, and the lizard. But as he meditates, his horse's hoofs clink among broken pottery, and, if he will but bend from his saddle, he will see in profusion the fragments of the ware of the prehistoric tribes, specimens of varied form, both of indented ware and of quaint painted design. As he threads his way over the plain, he will note here and there the burial-mounds and the irrigating works of a departed people, and will find arrow-points and other relics in profusion.   As he wanders through cañons he will see, now upon the right, and again upon the left, long lines of steps and stairways leading to apparently inaccessible eyries upon the cliffs above.   Crowning the cliffs, and built upon the cañon's brink, he will catch sight of picturesque towers, from whose walls the primitive sentinels watched and guarded the approaches to peaceful valleys below.   Everywhere evidence will be given that savage warriors once struggled and battled for the possession of the land.

Of all the localities where ruins of cliff-dwellings are found, it is in southwestern Colorado and northern New Mexico that the best-preserved structures are to be met; and to circumscribe the limits still closer, it is in that section of Colorado which is embraced by the Mesa Verde, a plateau through which Mancos Cañon has cut its way, that the grandest as well as the most picturesquely situated ruins have been discovered.   This, in connection with the fact that this land of cañons and mesas is surrounded on the north and east by one of the most beautiful mountain chains in the world, renders the country a most fascinating field for the explorer.

It is proposed in this volume to give the record of two summers' personal experience amid the scenes once familiar to the eyes of the Cliff-Dwellers. Drawn thither both by a love for the mountains and cañons and by an amateur's interest in archæology, my narrative will include the twofold experience of the climber and the interested seeker for new archæological wonders. As no compact volume has as yet, so far as I am aware, presented the attractive story of the discovery and development of this novel country, I will venture to preface my descriptions with a short account of the advent of the Spaniards in the southwest, of their occupancy, and then later of the entrance of our own countrymen upon the scene, together with some discussion of the wild tribes and pueblo towns as found by the early explorers, or as observed more recently by visiting students of archæology. If the reader thinks that some of these matters have little connection with the story of the vanished people and their ruins and relics, let him remember that the early explorers and settlers hovered closely about the Land of the Cliff-Dwellers. Though they rarely penetrated within its borders, their experiences are of interest as increasing our knowledge of the country and its inhabitants. We may infer that the nomads of the desert plains, mountain valleys, and rugged cañons, the ancestors of those encountered by Pike and the pioneers of the Santa Fé trail, influenced the destinies of the Cliff-Dwellers; while some of the dwellers in fixed habitations are possibly the direct descendants of the Men of the Cliff.

CHAPTER II.

A LARGE, increasing, and interesting literature has grown up pertaining to the geology, geography, and archæology of the Southwest.
The archæology, however, bears more especially
upon the inhabited pueblos, such as those of the
Taos, Moqui, and Zuñi Indians,— races known
in early times to the Spaniards through rumors
brought to the ears of Nuño de Guzman in 1530,
when he was at the head of affairs in Mexico.[1]

Before this date, though Cortez and his followers had heard legends of Amazons who were
supposed to dwell to the north of Mexico,[2] it
does not appear that they had heard of the semi-
civilized tribes of the North, and it was an Indian
slave of Guzman's who first gave reports that im-
pelled that leader to undertake an expedition to

---

[1] Narrative and Critical History of America, edited by Justin
Winsor, article Early Exploration of New Mexico, by Henry W.
Haynes, vol. ii. pp. 474 *et seq.*
[2] Bandelier, vol. v. pp. 1 and 2.

prove the truth of the stories, and possibly to extend his domain. Guzman was at enmity with Cortez, and was anxious to accomplish some great work that should gain him favor at the Spanish court. Tejos, the Indian slave, whose father was a trader among the Indians, stated that he had accompanied him, and seen cities equal to Mexico itself, where gold and silver were abundant. The allurement was so strong that Guzman organized an expedition to explore the Far North. His force amounted to four hundred Spaniards and twenty thousand Indians [1] On account of the difficulties which beset their path, the army did not reach a point beyond Colombo, and then returned. Guzman now disappears from the history of the Southwest; the new viceroy, Antonio de Mendoza, superseded him with Vasquez de Coronado.

Mendoza was a man of great sagacity and capacity. He was anxious to extend the domain of New Spain; and now came news through a channel which gave another impulse to Northern exploration.[2] Antonio Nuñez Cabeza de Vaca arrived upon the scene, and his name blazed out in the annals of the Southwest. He was with

[1] Winsor, vol. ii. p. 472. Bancroft, vol. xv. p. 28, gives the force as five hundred Spaniards and ten thousand allies

[2] Winsor, vol. ii. p. 474.

Narvaez' ill-fated expedition, most of whose members were lost or scattered in Florida or along the northern coast of the Gulf of Mexico. After many adventures and much wandering, he found himself west of the Mississippi. With three companions, Dorantes, Maldonado, and a negro named Estevan, he made his way westward to the Pacific coast. His route lay far south of the pueblo homes; but in some part of his journey rumors reached him of cities to the north either still existing or in ruins; and, on reaching the Spanish settlements, adventurers there were incited to further efforts to explore what is now known as New Mexico.[1]

This information being transmitted to Mendoza, he communicated the same to Coronado, who in 1539 organized a preliminary expedition. As guide he secured the services of Estevan, the negro who had been one of Cabeza de Vaca's comrades. The Franciscan monks, eager to propagate the Catholic faith, sent two of their number, Fray Marcos and Fray Honoratos. These three were accompanied by some natives who had followed Cabeza de Vaca to Mexico. It is stated that the small party were thus enabled to converse with the tribes among whom they were to dwell,

[1] Bandelier, vol. v. pp. 25 et seq.

and through whose country they were to pass. The party grew in numbers as it advanced, and after many adventures the negro Estevan, who proceeded some days in advance of the monks, reached the famed Seven Cities of Cibola. Estevan was murdered, and Fray Marcos, after viewing the pueblos from a distance, withdrew, and returned to Compostello.

From Fray Marcos' report we have our first knowledge of the New Mexican pueblos, and upon his return Coronado organized a new expedition, which penetrated into New Mexico, and finally, in search of the mythical city of Quivira, far beyond to the land of the Pawnees in Kansas and Nebraska. The prime cause of this invasion was a thirst for gold and riches, which the stories of the Indian Tejos and the reports of Fray Marcos (who, however, had no intention of fraud) led them to believe were to be found in the land of the Seven Cities of Cibola. These treasure-seekers were doomed to disappointment.[1]

Coronado's army found things entirely different from what was expected. Where populous towns

---

[1] Winsor, vol. ii. p. 475 *et seq.* For an interesting study of the journey of Fray Marcos, see Bandelier, vol. v. chap. iv. According to this authority, the priest has been much maligned, and has further suffered at the hands of his translators.

were supposed to exist, ruins were found, and when Cibola was reached, the disappointment was still greater. The natives were hostile, and it became necessary to carry the pueblos by storm. This was soon accomplished, though in the assault the leader nearly lost his life. The Spaniards found their armor of service, for it·protected them from the stones which were hurled down upon them from the terraced buildings. None of the Spaniards were killed, though some were wounded, and they lost a few horses.

The Moqui towns were explored from this point by Pedro de Tobar. This province was reduced. Here the Spaniards heard of the Colorado River, and Garcia Lopez de Cardenas was sent to explore it.[1] Melchior Diaz also explored the Colorado River nearer to its source, and gave it the name Rio del Tizon. In this expedition he lost his life.[2]

Besides Cibola and Tusayan, Coronado's forces visited Tiguex, Cicuye, and Acoma. At Tiguex, troubles with the natives resulted in a hard fight.[3]

---

[1] Winsor, vol. ii. pp. 480–484; Bandelier, vol. v. chap. iv. pp. 106 et seq.

[2] Bancroft, vol. xvii. p. 39.

[3] Winsor, pp. 490 et seq.

Coronado did not linger long in the pueblo country, for rumors reached the army of the existence of a city called Quivira, which lay far across the plains to the northeast; and his forces took up their march in that direction. The army was under the guidance of a lying native whom the Spaniards, from his resemblance to the people of the Bosphorus, called "the Turk." This Indian claimed to be a native of a country a thousand miles to the eastward, and told fabulous stories of Quivira and its gold and silver.[1] An Indian named Xabe partially corroborated the stories of El Turco; but another Indian guide, Sopete, who accompanied Coronado's expedition, pronounced "the Turk" a falsifier. The adventurers did not place much reliance upon the stories of Sopete, for the Querechos, a tribe of the Apaches, confirmed the statements of the romancer.[2]

Coronado's army left the banks of the Rio Grande on May 5, 1541. For days and days the troops marched across the plains. Wandering bands of Querechos and Teyas were met with. These people lived in tents of skin, and hunted the buffalo to gain subsistence. In the middle of

[1] Bancroft, vol. xvii. pp. 51, and Prince, History of New Mexico, p. 129.

[2] Bancroft, vol. xvii. p. 60.

June the main army, under Arellanno, was left behind, and soon returned to New Mexico, while Coronado, with some threescore selected followers, pursued the onward march. Immense herds of buffalo were passed, which seemed to increase in numbers as progress was made inland. The army finally reached Quivira, which turned out to be a collection of Indian villages composed of huts or wigwams of straw. The tribes occupying them are supposed to have been the Pawnees.[1] Discomfited by the results of the expedition, Coronado returned to New Mexico. There he met with an accident, which soon afterwards caused him to return to New Spain.

Thus we have an account of an expedition crossing the entire Western border, and skirting the eastern base of the Rocky Mountains. This was in 1541, seventy-nine years before the Pilgrims landed on Plymouth Rock, and a few years before Cabrillo pushed his way up the California coast to latitude 44°[2] For a period of a century and three quarters the sources of information of this section of the country are principally Castañeda's report of this invasion. Even in the early part of

---

[1] Prince, History of New Mexico, pp. 140 etc.; Bancroft, vol. xvii. pp. 61 etc.; Simpson's Coronado's March.

[2] Bancroft, vol. xxvii.; Hist. Northwest Coast, vol. i. p. 14.

this century, European cyclopædists have nothing to add in the way of information in regard to what is now the geographical centre of the United States. Lengthy articles on the Pacific States grace their pages, yet the mighty ranges of the central Cordilleras are barely mentioned as the Stony Mountains. The chain was described as a prolongation of the Andes, and the designation "Stony" considered inappropriate. Acknowledging that little was known, the writers stated that the range rose in northern New Mexico and reached the Arctic Ocean. They slurred Pike's reports and belittled the value of his work, because his expedition was scantily supplied with philosophical instruments. The plains at the base of the mountains were supposed to be about thirty-five hundred feet above the sea, and the peaks supposed to rise to the same altitude above the sandstone floor, — this, upon the authority of Humboldt, who guessed that the altitude was between six thousand and seven thousand feet above sea-level. He conjectured within fifty per centum of the true values.[1]

After Coronado's expedition, two Franciscan monks, with Chamuscado, a miner, with others, ventured into New Mexico. This was in 1581.

[1] Edinburgh Encyclopædia, 1832, vol. xv. p. 565.

They visited the pueblo districts, where the
friars remained. They died as martyrs to their
faith.

In 1582, in order to discover the fate of the
missing monks, Espejo organized an expedition on
his own account to explore New Mexico. At the
pueblo towns he received information of the previous visit of Coronado. At Zuñi (Cibola) were
found Indians who had accompanied Coronado
forty years previous. Espejo also went to Moqui,
and visited in all seventy-four pueblos. He gave
the population as two hundred and fifty thousand, which is unquestionably far above the
true number. The results of Espejo's expedition,
accompanied as he was by but fifteen persons,
were of as much importance as those obtained
by Coronado with his great army.[1]

About 1595 we have partial records of another
Spanish expedition. Captain Bonilla was sent
against the Indians of the plains; but dazzled by
reports of wealth among the northern tribes, he
exceeded his instructions and took his way toward
the Missouri. The Spanish governor of Vizcaya
(northern Mexico) sent Cazorla to order him
home; but the buccaneer heeded not, and in an
altercation with a subordinate named Humaña,

[1] Bancroft, vol. xvii. chap. iv.

the leader was killed, and the victor took command of the troop. The narrative states that they
crossed a broad river on a raft. At this juncture
three Indians who had accompanied the expedition from New Mexico deserted. Only one of
these reached the settlements again, and informed
Oñate, the governor, of the affair. While the
on-going party were encamped on the plains, a
large force of Indians set fire to the grass and
then attacked them, destroying all but Alonzo
Sanchez and a half-breed girl. Afterwards the
natives made Sanchez a chief. All that we know
of this doubtful part of the story comes from
him.[1]

[1] Bancroft, vol. xvii. p. 108.

CHAPTER III.

SPANISH OCCUPANCY.

DURING the closing years of the sixteenth century, New Mexico was actually taken possession of by the Spaniards. The leader was Juan de Oñate. His wife was Isabel, a granddaughter of Cortez, and a great-granddaughter of Montezuma. The greatest resistance to the Spaniards was at Acoma, where the battle lasted two days. On account of their weapons and armor, the loss of the Spaniards was slight. Many of the Indians were killed, and the pueblo was finally surrendered.[1] The natives generally were found comparatively friendly, though one of them,

[1] Bancroft, vol. xvii. chapter vii. ; Oñate's Conquest, pp. 128 *et seq.* Capt. John G. Bourke, in his delightful book, "On the Border with Crook," describes a suit of armor in his possession which was undoubtedly worn by a Spanish soldier of the sixteenth century. It was found some twenty years ago near the Rio Grande. The skeleton of the owner was in the armor. Bourke considers that the armor belonged to a soldier of Espejo's or Oñate's expedition. Later the Spaniards used the cotton-batting covering of the Aztecs, which was light in weight, and offered sufficient protection against arrows.

Zutucapan, endeavored to raise a general conspiracy against the invaders.

Colonists now thronged in, bringing with them
cattle, horses, and sheep, and in 1601 Oñate led
an expedition across the prairie, which occupied
the season from June until October. Travelling
northeast, he reached latitude 39° or 40°   Santa
Fé was founded at some time between the years
1605 and 1616. It is stated that in 1617 the
friars had built eleven churches and converted
fourteen thousand natives.[1]

It is stated that when the Spaniards becàme
thoroughly intrenched in their position, many of
the natives were forced into slavery and compelled to work in mines. Doubt has been cast
upon the assertion that mines were worked by the
aborigines or by the Spaniards in these early days.
It is probable that the aborigines confined themselves largely to the mining of free metals. Silver was obtained near the surface at a number of
mines. Gold and copper were found in a similar
manner, and in such condition that they could be
hammered into varied forms. But there is some
evidence to show that the Spaniards, after con-

[1] It is sometimes stated that Santa Fé is the oldest city in
the United States ; but this is not so : compare St. Augustine,
founded about 1565.

quering the natives, forced them to work mines, and that after the successful rebellion of the pueblos, these mines were closed.[1] I am indebted to my friend Dr. F. M. Endlich, formerly connected with Hayden's Survey, and at present manager of the Yankee Boy Mining Co., of Ouray, for the following interesting bit of information :—

In the neighborhood of Cook's Peak in New Mexico he started to open up some lead mines. After having driven a tunnel to about eighty feet, he sank a winze from the same to a depth of about twenty feet. One day the winze, and the men in it, suddenly disappeared. There was a commotion in camp, and upon investigation it was found that the bottom of the winze had

[1] I am aware that this is heresy, — an opinion that is in conflict with that held by the best authorities ; still, so many American and Mexican tribes used and wrought the precious metals that I see no reason why the Pueblo Indians, or at least the Spaniards of that day, might not have discovered and worked mines, if only to a limited extent. See foot-note, p. 50, in regard to the Navajo silver-workers. Also compare articles by Carl Lumholtz in "Scribner's Magazine," vol. x., November, 1891, p. 583, and Bulletin of the American Geographical Society, vol. xxiii. p. 388. This writer calls attention to the rumored existence of the mines of Vajnopa and Tayopa in the Sierra Madre of northern Mexico, which were owned by the Jesuits. "According to tradition, the Apaches killed every soul in these two mines." These mines, the existence of which is revealed by the study of Church records and Spanish documents, have been entirely forgotten, and await re-discovery.

dropped out, and that the men had been carried with sliding dirt a distance of seventy feet. Further examination showed that these seventy feet were an old stope containing Indian potsherds and stone tools; no trace of metal tools was found. The superintendent then abandoned that portion of the mine, and went farther up hill to sink a shaft on the same vein, at a spot where stood a juniper-tree apparently two or three hundred years old. He had the tree cut down, sank a shaft, and in eighteen feet struck ancient workings again.

Apart from the native metals, the ores which the Spaniards particularly sought were carbonates of lead, — ores which they thoroughly understood and were accustomed to smelt. Many a mine in Arizona and New Mexico bears traces of old Spanish workings. Lead mines, however, furnished a much better material for the reduction of silver, which was one of the perquisites beyond all others of the Spanish conquerors.

In time the Spanish rule became oppressive, and several of the friars who had established missions at the pueblo towns were murdered. About 1672 the Apaches invaded the district, destroyed several of these towns, and some of the friars were killed. In time, the pueblos revolted against their foreign masters, and succeeded in driving them away. Hundreds of the Spaniards were massacred, and the survivors fled into the southern valleys. The leader of the natives was named Pope. After the retreat of the Spaniards, the Estufas (the Council and Religious Chambers of the pueblos) were re-opened, and the churches and crosses were destroyed. In 1692 the country was re-conquered by Diego de Vargas, and the power of the pueblo tribes, as far as united effort was concerned, was forever crushed. From 1687 to 1711 the Jesuit Father Eusebio Francisco Kino accomplished much in the way of establishing missions in Sonora, near the borders of Arizona, and paved the way for the sway of the monks. [1]

In 1698 the Spaniards feared invasion by the French from Louisiana, and in 1700 the Apaches told of an Indian village that had been destroyed by them.[2] In 1719 Valverde, with over a hundred Spaniards, and with the assistance of the Apaches, waged strife with the Yutahs and Comanches. In this warfare he skirted the eastern base of the Rocky Mountains, and is thought to have reached a more northern point than any of the

[1] Bancroft, vol. xvii. pp. 352-354.
[2] La Salle discovered the mouth of the Mississippi in 1682, and was murdered in Texas in 1687.

previous explorers. On the banks of a river, probably the Arkansas, he came upon men who had received gunshot wounds at the hands of the French or their Indian allies. It was about this time that all the country west of the Mississippi was claimed by the French. The same year that Valverde crossed the plains, Du Tissenet was sent from New Orleans to explore the regions to the north.[1] Doubtless it was his expedition that was reported by the Indians of the plains to the Spanish on the frontier of New Mexico, and we learn that they sent a caravan fron Santa Fé in the following year to put a stop to the encroachments of the French. Historians do not entirely agree in stating the facts in regard to this expedition. Some write that the Spaniards blundered,[2] and that the Missouri Indians, who were friendly to the French, treacherously fell upon them and destroyed all but one man, a priest, who escaped to Santa Fé and preserved the records.

From this time on, till the coming of the Americans, the history of the Spanish occupancy is made up of details of the misrule of the priests and the sorrowful story of Indian wars. But in a country where, on account of climatic conditions,

[1] Bancroft, vol. xvii. p. 222.
[2] Holloway, History of Kansas, p. 88 ; Spring, Kansas, p. 20.

wants were few, the people, by the aid of irrigation, without any very hard labor and with the
help of their burros, sheep, and cattle, eked out
a comfortable subsistence. A system of serfdom
called "peonage" (voluntary servitude for debt)
grew up, and thus the cattle and sheep owners
were able to have their herds taken care of at
little expense.[1]

[1] Scribner's Magazine, vol. x., No. 6, p. 769, — C. F.
Lummis.

CHAPTER IV.

ANGLO-AMERICAN EXPLORATION.

THERE is some evidence that an Indian of the Missouri valley traversed the country to the waters of the Columbia, and between the years 1745 and 1750 descended that great river to the Pacific. This is the only case where we learn of an Indian finding a transcontinental pathway. If the report is true, he forestalled even the French of Canada, for it was not until 1752 that there was established a fort at the base of the Rockies in British Columbia, and not until 1793 did Mackensie cross the Northern Rockies and the Canadian Selkirks,[1] though he thus anticipated by some twelve years those adventurous travellers from within our own borders, Lewis and Clarke.

Not a trapper from our own frontier had even reached the base of the Rockies before 1800. Is it not strange that, with New Mexico, the Pacific States, even parts of the bleak Alaskan shores, comparatively well known, with the French trap-

[1] Bancroft, Northwest Coast, vol. i. (xxvii.) pp. 26, 28.

pers girdling the continent in British America, and La Vérendrye sighting the mountains about the sources of the Yellowstone, nevertheless the great Central Plain and the highway through South Pass were entirely unknown? No white man had ever looked upon the great peaks of the Front and Wind River ranges. Perhaps it is not strange that the Canadians extended their frontier so much faster than the Americans, for they controlled the great highway by the Lakes; while we know that when the first Continental Congress assembled, there were but two or three hundred Americans west of the Alleghanies,[1] and even at the end of the war of the Revolution the greater part of what is now the United States was under the dominion of Spain.

The first man to reach the Rockies by the way of the Platte River was La Lande from Kaskaskia. Between Louisiana and New Mexico there had been no trading communications before 1800, though both parties had established flourishing commerce with the Indians. But in 1804 William Morrison of Kaskaskia sent Baptiste La Lande, a French creole, with merchandise, directing him to reach Santa Fé if possible, and to establish trade at that point.

[1] Roosevelt, The Winning of the West, vol. ii. p. 370.

He succeeded in reaching the Rockies, and meeting with Indians, despatched them to Santa Fé
with the news of the arrival of a merchant from
the Far East. Being well received, he disposed
of his goods at fabulous prices, and, charmed by
some lovely brunettes of the town, he decided to
remain in the country; and leaving his employer
to whistle for his money, appropriated the gains
of his journey.[1]

In 1802 a Kentuckian, James Purseley, and two
hunters set out from the Mississippi for a hunting expedition on the Osage River. The Kansas
Indians stole their horses, but by heroic efforts
Purseley recovered at least his own. The next
year we find him with a horde of Indians hunting and trading on the Platte. The Sioux uncere-
moniously drove this mixed assemblage into the
mountains. They finally reached the northern
boundary of New Mexico, and Purseley went
ahead to feel the pulse of the Spaniards. He was
received by Governor Alencaster in a friendly
manner, and the whole band, following after,
spent considerable time in satisfactory trade.

---

[1] Bancroft, vol. xvii. p. 291 ; Prince, History of New Mexico,
p. 267 ; Bancroft, vol. xxv. p. 351. Two trappers, Workman
and Spencer, were the first Americans to cross the Rockies south
of Lewis and Clarke's Pass.

Purseley had had enough of the savages, and decided to rest at Santa Fé. He had found gold on the tributaries of the Platte, and carried some of the grains in his shot-pouch for many months, but finally threw the sample away. Having casually alluded to the subject to some Spaniards, they urged him to show them the place of discovery. He refused, perhaps for patriotic reasons, thinking the land belonged to his own countrymen instead of to the New Mexicans. He afterwards told the truth to Lieutenant Pike.[1]

Rumors of intended exploration on the part of the United States, and reports that the Burr conspiracy might change the Spanish frontier, led the Spaniards in 1806 to send Lieutenant Melgares, with a force of one hundred dragoons, from Chihuahua, — not to fight the Indians of the plains, but to conciliate them. This commander was joined by five hundred militia. He descended the Red River, took counsel of the Comanches, who had been practically useful in giving information of the intentions of the Americans, and then crossed northward to the Arkansas. He visited the nation of the Pawnees, presented the tribesmen with medals and flags, and gave a commission to their head chief. It is unfortunate that

[1] Prince, History of New Mexico, pp. 268–270.

this little army could not have been captured by the United States troops just as Pike's force was afterwards entrapped by the New Mexicans on the headwaters of the Rio Grande. Melgares afterwards returned by the Arkansas to the Rocky Mountains, and thence to Santa Fé.[1] In this expedition no American explorers or filibusters were met with ; but considering the great distance travelled, this survey of territory rivals in importance the journeys of Lewis and Clarke, and that of Pike.[2]

Lieutenant Pike, after his journey to the sources of the Mississippi, took command, at the request of his chief, General Wilkinson, of an expedition to the Rockies. In the middle of October, 1805, he caught glimpses of the Rocky Mountains, and afterwards, among its snows, encountered many hardships. On the 3d of December he measured the height of the mountain to which his name had been given, and which will keep his memory constantly before his countrymen. He soon afterwards crossed the thirty-eighth parallel, and found himself and his followers in New Mexican territory, and, as prisoners, led to Santa Fé.[3]

[1] Bancroft, vol. xvii. pp. 285-286 ; Prince, History of New Mexico, p. 248.

[2] Prince, p. 248.

[3] Prince, pp. 249-252 ; Bancroft, vol. xxv. p. 344, and vol. xxvii. pp. 293-296.

Now that these preliminary journeys of La Lande, Purseley, and Pike were known, trade with Santa Fé began; especially from the information brought by the intrepid Pike was attention called to the possible profits to be gained in such traffic. The oncoming American trader had this great advantage, that he was much nearer to New Mexico than his Southern competitors. The only other route by which goods could be received was by sea to Vera Cruz, thence overland to the city of Mexico, then by a tedious route to El Paso, and finally by caravans which once in six months travelled up the Rio Grande.[1]   Trade with Santa Fé gradually increased; but on account of the hostility of the Indians, an armed escort was furnished by the Government.[2] Previous to 1822, pack-mules only were used for the Santa Fé trade; but in that year wagons were introduced.   The trail became definitely marked in 1834, for during that season rain was continuous and the turf soft, so that the wagon-wheels cut deep ruts on the line of the most direct route, and these marks, deepened from year to year, were never obliterated while this route was used.[3]   The wagons were drawn by

---

[1] Prince, p. 271.

[2] Gregg, Commerce of the Prairies, vol. i. pp. 29, 30, 31.

[3] Ibid., p. 311 (Philadelphia, 1851).

mules or oxen. The distance from Council Grove to Santa Fé was about 625 miles; the transit consumed about forty days. At first single parties ventured alone on the long journey; but as the Indian troubles thickened, it was customary for several "outfits" to join in one caravan. The stories of these adventurers are as interesting as the tale of any border life. Strange and dangerous as was such a career, participants were ever attracted back again to the free life on the broad prairie. The excitement and novelty of meeting the different tribes of Indians on the route, the chase of the buffalo, the stalking of the antelope, and the many novel sights and sounds tended to fascinate all who loved adventure. Stories of this trail through Kansas to Santa Fé have furnished facts for Mayne Reid and Marryat. Beside the animals indigenous to the plains the wild horse now took a place, and marvellous stories were told of the milk-white steed with black-tipped ears, the fleetest animal of the broad plains, that was the leader of one of the bands, that distanced all pursuers.[1] About this time trappers and hunters came to occupy a prominent place in the annals

[1] Gregg, vol. ii. p. 207. This is an interesting bit of folklore described by Gregg. Within a few years I have heard similar stories in different parts of the West.

of the region, some of them acting in the capacity of guides to various exploring parties. Among these was the famous Kit Carson.[1]

Now forts and trading posts began to be established near the base of the Rockies,—the Bents, St. Vrain and others being interested in the large fur-trade. Some of these structures, built for defence, were made of adobe, imitating the style of Mexican and pueblo architecture.[2]

The Mexicans had a farming establishment,

---

[1] Though living in my youth in a frontier town, one of the termini of the Santa Fé trail, my experience in the Rockies has been with the second generation of guides and hunters. William Carson, a son of the preceding, was my companion once in the Sangre de Cristo Mountains. Following his father's vocation for some years, he was a scout in campaigns against the Utes; but after the close of Indian warfare he settled down at Fort Garland, near Sierra Blanca. Since my trip with him he has met his death, caused by the accidental discharge of a pistol.

[2] H. H. Bancroft, History of Nevada, Colorado, and Wyoming, vol. xxv. This writer quotes (p. 354) from Farnham's "Travels in the Great Western Prairies," p. 35 : "The author of this book was at Fort William in 1839, and wrote accurately of what he saw."

"In the months of June, August, and September there are in the neighborhood of those traders from fifteen thousand to twenty thousand savages ready and panting for plunder and blood. If they engage in battling out old causes of contention among themselves, the Messrs. Bent feel comparatively safe in their solitary fortress. But if they spare each other's property and lives, there are great anxieties at Fort William ; every hour of day and night is pregnant with danger."

connected with the trading post, called El Pueblo. This was located where the Colorado city of Pueblo now stands.[1]   Grants of large tracts of land were made to private individuals by the Mexican Government; such are the claims known as the Beaubien,[2] Vigil, St. Vrain, and Luis Maria Baca grants. The last-named is now known as "The Gilpin Ranch," its later owner having acquired it by purchase.   It is situated in San Luis Park, the fertile lands lying under the shadow of the mighty Sangre de Cristo range, the noble Crestone Peak being included in the alpine domain.   The northern border of the ranch lies along the thirty-eighth parallel, which formerly marked the southern limits of the United States territory in this section of country.   This boundary line is now marked by a barbed wire fence.[3]

[1] For a vivid account of this post, see "Lippincott's Magazine," December, 1880, "Historical Rocky Mountain Outpost," by George Rex Buckman.

[2] Bancroft, vol. xxv. p. 594.   Lucien Maxwell married Beaubien's daughter and purchased the great tract of land. "He erected a fine house on the Cimarron, where he entertained in good old feudal style, surrounded by his dependents, and owning immense herds of cattle, sheep, and blooded horses, employing as herders all the Cimarrons."

[3] One of my companions in many ascents of the Rockies once remarked of this fence, "One could not fail to run his eye with interest along the wire fence that marked its northern limit, when told that it was on the thirty-eighth parallel.   For once a

In 1821 Mexico, under the leadership of Itur-
bide, a native Mexican, gained independence from
Spain. In 1824 the republic was organized, which
in a few years was recognized by the United
States. In 1846 war was declared against Mexico
by the United States, and General Kearney
marched with a small army towards Santa Fé.
It is not any part of this book to discuss politi-
cal events, but let us consider for a moment the
race of people whom he was to oppose. We have
been regarding the conquerors of Mexico and
of the lands to the north as Spaniards; we must
now speak of them as Mexicans, — and a strange
people they were. The inhabitants of the Spanish
peninsula had had engrafted into their stock
many foreign elements. Originally Iberians and
Celts, their lands were overrun by Vandals and
Visigoths. Later the followers of Mahomet,
in impetuous westward movements, overran
northern Africa, and a Mohammedan people, the
Moors, conquered Spain. For several centuries
these Southern people lived in the conquered
land, and though expelled in the fourteenth cen-

parallel of latitude seemed to have a tangible existence, — if a
barbed wire fence can be called 'tangible'" ("Appalachia,"
vol. v. p. 267: "Through San Luis Park to Sierra Blanca," by
Charles E. Fay).

tury, their blood was mingled with that of the
fairest chivalry of Spain. So among the Spanish
conquerors in the New World were many knights
whose ancestors had been followers of the Prophet,
descendants of men who from the house-tops, and
with their faces turned towards Mecca, called upon
the name of Allah.

Here in the land of the pueblos we find these
descendants of the Moors, living in a land which
may be compared in many ways to Arabian
and African deserts, and, under the shadow of a
mightier Sierra Madre than they saw in Spain,
intermingling with and marrying the daughters
of pueblo chiefs, of a race who also from the terraces upon the house-tops made their prayers,
and with their faces turned towards the east
worshipped the rising sun.[1]

The history of the easy conquest of New
Mexico by the Americans is well known, and
the report of how the Mexicans ran away has
impressed upon our own people the opinion that

[1] Castañeda chronicles that the pueblos had aged priests,
persons who at sunrise ascended to the highest terraces of the
villages, there to a silent and reverential people delivered a
sermon, and gave them counsel on the way of living (Ternaux-
Compans, vol. ix., "Relation").

Also compare "A Journal of American Ethnology and Archæology," J. Walter Fewkes, editor, vol. i. pp. 3, 4, 5.

they were a cowardly race. Is it probable that a people descended from such renowned world-finders as were the Spanish cavaliers of only three centuries ago should have so degenerated ? Is it not more likely that the weakness of the New Mexicans was due to the quality of their leadership, and to the fact that there was little to bind them to the central government far in the south ? [1]

After the American annexation, the country was visited by travellers and scientific observers. Well-equipped expeditions, sent out by the United States Government, explored many remote corners, and the results as portrayed in different reports give us much information in regard to the archæology of this fascinating land.

Later the Bureau of Ethnology placed special investigators in the field, and their work is being recorded in beautifully illustrated volumes.[2]

[1] This is the view of the Mexican character which is taken by Davis in ''El Gringo,'' and by other authorities. For an interesting sketch of New Mexico and its people of the present day, I would refer the reader to an article, by C. F. Lummis, in '' Scribner's Magazine'' for December, 1891. ''Sun, silence, and adobe,— that is New Mexico in three words . . . Here is the land of *poco tiempo* — the home of ' Pretty Soon.' Why hurry with the hurrying world ? The ' pretty soon ' of New Spain is better than the ' Now ! Now !' of the haggard States. The opiate sun soothes to rest, the adobe is made to lean against, the hush of day-long noon would not be broken.''

[2] On account of the already too great length of these historical

notes, I will not attempt to follow in detail the records of different exploring parties. It is sufficient that I refer and quote from them in the following pages, and at present simply mention some of them : —

John R. Bartlett, " Personal Narrative of Explorations," etc.; Capt. L. Sitgreaves, " Report of an Expedition to the Zuñi and Colorado Rivers ; " Lieut. J. W. Abert, " Report of his Examination of New Mexico ; " Lieut.-Col. W. H. Emory, " Journal of a Military Reconnoissance;" J. W. Powell, " Exploration of the Colorado of the West ; " Reports of Lieutenant Ives, Lieut. J. H. Simpson, Dr. Oscar Leow, Lieutenants Whipple and Birnie ; " Report upon United States Geographical Surveys," First Lieut. Geo. M. Wheeler. In vol. vii. (Archæology) is a valuable report on the pottery and relics of the Southwest, by Frederick W. Putnam.

Of the workers in the ranks of the Bureau of Ethnology staff (those especially connected with the field work), mention may well be made of Mr. F. H. Cushing, widely known also for his Zuñi studies, through many magazine articles (" The Century," vol. xxiv. pp. 526, " An Aboriginal Pilgrimage," and vol. xxv. p. 191, 500, " My Adventures in Zuñi ") ; Mr. W. H. Holmes, whose writings upon pottery and other subjects are of the greatest value ; Victor Mindeleff; Cosmo Mindeleff ; and Mr. Hillers, the competent photographer.

CHAPTER V.

WILD TRIBES.

ALL through the broad land covered by Coronado's march were found scattered either wild tribes or a semi-civilized people. Let us speak first of the former.

In the southwest the Seris Indians were met with. They were by nature very fierce, and at times made havoc among the sedentary Indians of Sonora. In their warfare they used poisoned arrows.[1] The Tephuanas were ferocious savages, who cut off the heads of their stronger captives, and took the weaker ones for slaves. The

[1] That the Opates used them is fully established, and the counter-poison is also known. The custom appears to have been general with the tribes of Sonora, and the poison is described as mortal, though not in every instance. In addition to the bow and arrow, the usual and well-known aboriginal weapons, the club, the shield, and possibly the sling, were handled by the Opates in warfare, and, like less sedentary tribes, they frequently set out in small war-parties, accompanied by a sorcerer or medicine-man. — *Bandelier*, vol. iii. p. 70.

Opates used poisoned arrows and fortified elevated places, as is shown by remains in Sonora. The Tobosos of Chihuahua were also a very fierce people. [1]

Farther to the north, within the present limits of Mexico and Arizona, lived the Apaches, — a nomad people who warred continually. The Apaches are of Tinneh stock, and the name by which we know them is not a word of their tongue, but was given to them by the Maricopas and passed over to us by the Mexicans. Their ancestors occupied lands in the frozen north, in British America, where they were a peaceable people. But after emigration to a more southern clime, the branch in Arizona and New Mexico became fighters, and being of a very wild nature, they have been able until very recently to hold their own against all comers. [2] From the date of the arrival of the Spaniards till the conquest by General Crook, the Apaches have been at enmity against the whites. [3] Of the several bands, the Tonto Apaches were the fiercest. [4] The Apache used primitive weapons, such as the

---

[1] Bandelier, vol. iii. pp. 74, 76, 82, 94, 95.
[2] Bourke, On the Border with Crook, pp. 113, 114.
[3] Ibid., p. 2.
[4] Ibid., p. 129.

bow, arrow, and lance. He was clad very lightly, and he knew how to subsist upon the herbs and fruits of the country. Though in the western sections large game was scarce, wild turkeys, quails, and rabbits were plentiful.[1] A plant called the mescal was one of the main supplies of food. The Apaches have remarkably clear vision, and their mode of communication was by signal fires and smoke which shot up from the peaks and mesas. Dogs were used by them as beasts of burden. In the eastern section they lived almost entirely by the chase, continually following the buffalo.[2] This animal gave them meat, clothing, fuel, and shelter; from the bones they made their awls and arrow-points. The Apaches have intermarried with other tribes, especially with the Yumas and Mojaves. They ranged over a broad country, for Coronado met them in 1541 east of the pueblo of Pecos.

Like all other tribes, these Indians were very superstitious, and the medicine-man was an important character.

The Navajos, who were of the same stock as the Apaches, lived in the northern part of what

[1] Bourke, On the Border with Crook, pp. 129, 146.
[2] Bandelier, vol. iii. pp. 82, 178.

is now New Mexico. They formed a very powerful tribe. They state that they once came from
beyond the Sierra La Plata. They are a polyg-
amous people, but their religious creed is something like that of the pueblos. They irrigate the
land, till it, and live at times in log-cabins.[1]
They are blanket-weavers, and makers of pottery
and baskets.[2]

Among other tribes were the Mojaves, Yumas,
Hualapais, and Cosinos. Of these, the Hualapais
dwelt in and about the Grand Cañon of Colorado.
They were a brave people. Farther to the north
were the Yutahs, who occupied a broad country
in different branches, covering the whole of what
is now Utah and Colorado. In the West they
were a degraded race, much allied in habits and
customs to the Digger Indians.

On the eastern borders the Ute Indians, as

[1] Bancroft, vol. i. p. 596 ; Bandelier, vol. iii. pp. 175 and
288, also p. 31. In 1881 the population was estimated at
twenty-one thousand (Bandelier, vol. iii. p. 259; Bourke,
Snake-dance of the Moquis, p. 278; Bancroft, vol. xvii. p. 235).
The Comanches dwelling on the eastern plains do not appear in
history till 1716.

[2] The Navajo Indians of the present day are also silversmiths.
Many writers hold to the opinion that they did not learn the art
from Spaniards or Americans (2d Annual Report of the Bureau
of Ethnology for 1880-1881, article by Washington Matthews,
" Navajo Silversmiths ").

we are accustomed to speak of the tribes, formerly maintained their supremacy throughout
the greater part of that section of the Rocky
Mountains which lies in what is now known as
Colorado. From their fastnesses among these
sierras they frequently made incursions against
the Indians of the plains, and if unsuccessful in
such inroads, they retreated into rocky defiles
where it was destruction to their foes to pursue
them. The early Spanish expeditions met these
Yutahs on the prairie in their marches eastward
from the land of the pueblos. Till within a few
years the various tribes of this once great nation
hunted through the broad valleys of the San
Luis, South, and Middle Parks; traces of their
former habitations have but recently disappeared
from the banks of the river-courses in northern
Colorado, and their breastworks are still to be
met with on the eastern slopes of the San Juan
Mountains. At present the greater part of these
tribes, in diminished numbers, are confined to a
narrow strip of land, part of their ancient domain
in the southwestern corner of the State.

Of tribes somewhat in advance of the wandering Indians, mention may be made of the Pimas of
Arizona, the southern branch living in houses of
stone and adobe, and the more northern people

in huts. The Pimas wove cloth, tilled the soil, and were progressing in civilization when the Spaniards came. They irrigated the lands, not by digging canals, but by guiding mountain-torrents into their fields. [1]

[1] Bandelier, vol. iii. pp. 30, 104; Bancroft, vol. i. p. 529.

CHAPTER VI.

PUEBLO TRIBES.

THE Spanish invaders found nearly a hundred inhabited dwelling-places of the pueblo tribes. Of these towns, Zuñi, Acoma, Tiguas, Queres, Jemez, Tehua, and Taos are identified as places named in the Spanish chronicles.[1] Many others which must have been inhabited at the date of the invasion have since fallen into ruin, while some were destroyed by the Spaniards, and others by the Indians. From the distribution of these ruins, — many of which, such as those of Casa Grande on the Gila River in Arizona, were in a state of dilapidation when the Spaniards came, — one infers that these people had been declining in numbers for centuries, and had been unable to maintain their hold against more savage tribes, the more civilized going down before the more barbarous.[2]

The pueblo district proper occupied a country some two hundred and fifty miles from north to

[1] Bandelier, vol. i. p. 28.
[2] Bancroft, vol. xvii. pp. 3, 4.

south, and about three hundred miles from east to west. Of the towns, Taos was the most northern, and Moqui the westernmost. The villages were somewhat widely separated, and the inhabitants were often hostile. Wild tribes hunted over the intervening spaces, for the sedentary people occupied but little of the adjacent valleys.[1]

The Zuñi group, which consists of seven distinct pueblos, has been identified with the Seven Cities of Cibola of the Spaniards.[2] The Moqui towns also consisted of seven villages. The great pueblo of Pecos contained the largest population. Acoma was famous for its position upon a bold rock rising up from the plains, and has not changed during three centuries.[3] It is built on a barren

[1] Bandelier, vol. iii. pp. 119, 120. "The pueblos, besides, were not harmonious among themselves. Divided into seven distinct linguistic groups, the difference of languages created a barrier that often led to intertribal hostilities. Moreover, there was not even unbroken peace between the villages of the same stock. The villages of that time were on an average much smaller than those of to-day inhabited by Pueblo Indians ; but there was a greater number of them. The aggregate population of the pueblos in the sixteenth and seventeenth centuries did not exceed twenty-five thousand souls."

[2] About thirty miles to the eastward of Zuñi is El Moro, or Inscription Rock, the high mesa above it crowned with ruins. On this rock many travellers have carved their names, Diego de Vargas placing his there in 1692.

[3] Bandelier, vol. iii. pp. 133, 127 ; Bandelier, vol. i. pp. 14 to 16.

sandstone mesa, or plateau, some three hundred feet above the plain. The town can be approached only by two narrow and very steep paths. It has three parallel streets, and about six hundred inhabitants. The houses, built of adobe, are of two or three stories. There are no doors or windows in the first story, and the roof, by which alone an entrance can be gained to these structures, can be reached only by ladders. The surface of the mesa contains about ten acres, and there are about sixty or seventy houses; the doors open to the south. The people cook in earthen pots of their own manufacture. They make an unfermented bread, which they roll into thin wafers. They use spoons made of horn and wood; they have no furniture, and sleep under sheepskins. There are no springs upon this plateau, but there is an artificial tank 20×150 feet, which is four to five feet deep. In this they collect the melted snow in winter, and rain-water in the summer. A mission was founded here in 1628, and in 1680 a number of the Franciscan monks connected with it were murdered.[1]

Taos is more isolated from the rest of the world than any of the other pueblos, for it is walled in

[1] Wheeler's Report, vol. vii., Archæology; Oscar Leow, p. 325, etc.

by very high mountains. An annual fair has been held here for many years, to which the Indians and pueblos come to trade. The building is very large, rising in terraces to a height of seven stories. The whole is surrounded by an adobe wall. The people have a belief that at some time Montezuma will come over this peak on the back of an eagle, and that there will then be an end to all their sorrows ; and one man is supposed to watch for this event every day in the year, with his face turned toward the mountain.[1]

Most of the pueblo structures were built in the form of terraces, and placed upon the top of high, isolated plateaus. They could only be reached by winding, circuitous paths, in many cases steps being cut on the face of cliffs. The lower stories have no doors or windows, the upper stories being reached by ladders, as has been shown in the description of Taos, entrance being gained by holes in the roof. The rooms of the buildings were generally very small ; the chimneys were made of pieces of very large jars, or ollas. Each pueblo had one or more estufas, or underground chambers,

---

[1] For information regarding Taos, I am indebted to my friend Mr. G. P. D. Townsend, of Colorado Springs, who has visited that pueblo and obtained much information and many valuable photographs. The Montezuma myth I have referred to in another chapter.

usually circular in form, though often square, in which religious exercises or the councils of the chiefs were held. The rafters of the buildings were made of hewn timbers, which were undoubtedly cut with stone axes. The customs of the people were very simple. They dressed in cloths of cotton and tanned skins, though in some cases they went naked in winter and in summer. The Moqui tribes raised their own cotton, and wove their own garments.

Most of the Pueblo Indians speak languages which are entirely different from one another, though the people of Pecos spoke the language of the Jemez, and in recent times, after becoming greatly reduced, abandoned their own pueblos and took refuge with their kindred. Many of the pueblo towns, such as Isleta, Santo Domingo, and Laguna, have become Mexicanized; but others, as those of Zuñi, Moqui, and Taos, are still somewhat primitive, and the stories written by the old Spanish chroniclers agree very nearly with the accounts given by modern explorers.

For instance, from Castañeda, the chronicler of Coronado's expedition, we learn that the province of Cibola contained seven villages, the houses of which are three or four stories high, though in one of the villages there were some which reached as high as seven stories. The Indians were very intelligent, and dressed themselves with pieces of cloth resembling napkins. They had mantles made of feather or rabbit-skins and cotton stuffs ; they also made garments of well-tanned skin. The women wore a kind of mantle, which they fastened around the neck and passed under the right arm. They rolled their hair up behind their ears in the form of a wheel. According to Castañeda, many bears, lions, wild-cats, otters, and other wild animals infested the land. Very large turquoises were found there, but, as was generally the case, not in such quantities as the eager Spaniards expected. The houses were built in common, the women making the mortar and building the walls. The pueblos had no lime, but made a mixture of ashes, dirt, and coal ; and though they ran the houses four stories high, the walls were not more than three feet in thickness : these were coated with a mixture made from burned twigs, earth, and water. They also made a kind of rubble-stone from the same mixture.[1] The houses belonged to the women, and the estufas to the men, the women not being allowed to sleep in

[1] The Pueblo Indians of the present day also make bricks of mud mixed with straw, forming the mass in moulds of wood or other material. See illustration facing page 41.

the estufas, or even enter them, except when they had occasion to bring food to their husbands or sons. There were many rooms, which were kept very clean; some were designed for kitchens, and others for grinding grain. The women ground this grain upon stones, which were fastened into the masonry. One of them cracked the grain, the next one crushed it, and the third reduced it to powder. They made great quantities of flour at once. In making bread they wet up this flour with warm water, and made a thin paste which resembled wafers.[1]

In all these provinces were found pottery and vases of curious form and workmanship.

To-day many of the Pueblo Indians have embraced the Catholic religion, and the Moquis are about the only tribe among whom there are no permanent priests. But the people cling to many of their heathen rites. The pueblos hold their land in common, but for purposes of cultivation it is divided among families. They raise their crops entirely by irrigation. They own a great deal of stock, consisting of large herds of horses, mules, and sheep. They are a very orderly and industrious people, live in harmony with each

---

[1] Ternaux-Compans, Castañeda, "Relation du Voyage de Cibola," vol. ix. part 2d, chaps. iii., iv., v.

other, and there are no paupers among them. Their original weapons were the bow and arrow. They are a very brave people, and were generally more than a match for the wild Indians. They are very superstitious, and are firm believers in witchcraft in all its varieties.[1]

Tusayan, or the Moqui towns are more interesting than any other pueblos existing at the present day, because their inhabitants retain most of their primitive customs.

Some of their villages are very picturesque, placed as they are upon high plateaus, the struc-

[1] Mr. W. H. Davis, "El Gringo, or New Mexico and Her People," pp. 145, 146; Wheeler, vol. vii., Archæology, pp. 317, 320.

Mr. G. Thompson, topographer of the expedition, relates interesting facts in regard to the pueblos. He describes them as of medium height, erect and graceful in bearing, and in disposition cordial and jovial. "In figure and stature the people of the pueblos are noble-looking and beautifully formed." According to this authority, each pueblo town had its own art; some excelled in pottery-making, others in weaving: the Moquis were the song-makers. The people of Jemez even went to Tusayan and bought songs. In regard to the music of the pueblos, Dr. Fewkes has recently succeeded in placing upon record some of the songs of the Zuñis. On one of his expeditions he carried with him a phonograph, and exposed it to the singing of some of the tribe. Mr. Benjamin Ives Gilman has, with the aid of a harmonium, taken down this music, and some eighteen pages of it are published in the "Journal of American Ethnology and Archæology," vol. i.

tures being erected upon the very brink of precipices. These houses are built of rubble-stone of
all sizes, from two to ten inches in diameter, the
wall being plastered with mud. The average size
of the rooms is twelve feet by ten, and seven feet
high. As in Coronado's time, the women own the
houses, for they build them and keep them in repair. The crops also belong to them after they
are housed.[1]

The land in the valleys at the foot of the mesa
is owned by them in common, a member of the
tribe controlling a given section only while he
keeps it under cultivation. There are many estufas in the different villages, and in some of these
are pictures of animals, such as the antelope, and
on some walls are pictographs representing clouds
and rainfall. In some cases these colors were
red and blue. Green pigments were obtained
from carbonate of copper, and pitch from the piñon
tree. Black was from charcoal, yellow from yellow ochre found in the country, and the white
probably from kaolin.[2]

Pottery-making is an important industry among
these people, the old squaws doing most of the

[1] "The Snake-dance of the Moquis of Arizona," by John G.
Bourke, pp. 115, 261.
[2] Ibid., p. 120.

work. The paste is made of marl and clay, which is mixed with water and then with finely crushed fragments of old pottery. After being made into the desired form it is sun-dried and then baked. It is not glazed, though, on account of polishing and cleansing, it sometimes has this appearance.[1] Beautiful baskets are also made in Tusayan. As with other Indian tribes, there were numerous clans in all the pueblo villages. There are eighteen of these among the Moquis, bearing such names as the Eagle, Corn, Water, Bear, Deer, Coyote, Road-runner.[2]

The Moquis have many very singular customs, one of the more marvellous being the snake-dance, which has some religious significance, in which live rattlesnakes are carried in the mouths of the dancers. They are a very superstitious people, believing in witches and witchcraft, and sing hymns, ring bells, and make great noises to drive away the evil spirits, and they always wear a talisman or amulet. Their mythology and theology are very complex. They have many gods and idols.

---

[1] Bandelier, vol. iii. p. 162. This writer states, "The pueblo, however, knew how to impart a certain lustre or glaze to some of the decorations on his earthern ware, and this art is lost." I have picked up many fragments among cliff-dwellings that I considered as glazed ware.

[2] Bourke, Snake-dance, p. 117.

The idols are very rough in form, sometimes representing animals such as the bear or mountain lion, or grotesque figures.[1] The more ugly the deity, the more sacred it is in the eyes of the people. The cloud-god Oma-a is one of the more important, because, on account of the scarcity of rainfall, they pray oftener for this blessing than for any other. They have many sacred springs in their country, where they leave their votive offerings of sticks and prayer-plumes.[2]

Thus we have a picture of the pueblo tribes of the Southwest as given by the early Spanish invaders and recent American observers. We find, as compared with the wild tribes who roamed throughout the broad land, that they were a sedentary, peaceable people, trading with their neighbors and with the tribes of Sonora. Living as they did, in their almost inaccessible houses of

[1] Bourke, Snake-dance, p. 131. In Tegua they had wooden gods, which, after serving for this purpose, were given to the children to play with as dolls.

[2] For a book that will give a good idea of the life, customs, and beliefs of the primitive Pueblo Indians, I would refer the reader to that very interesting romance, "The Delight Makers," by Adolf F. Bandelier. In the preface, the author writes : "This story is the result of eight years spent in ethnological and archæological study among the Pueblo Indians of New Mexico. . . . By clothing sober facts in the garb of romance, I have hoped to make the 'truth about the Pueblo Indians' more accessible, and perhaps more acceptable, to the public in general."

stone and adobe, they were somewhat protected from the fierce Indians, for they could draw up their ladders at night, and sleep in comparative peace and security. As for their origin, little is known, for some of their traditions state that they came from the West, and other facts lead us to think that certain tribes, within a few centuries, occupied cañons to the north. Certain it is that some of them formerly dwelt in cave and cliff-houses in the cañons, and we have much reason to infer that the inhabitants of the two classes of dwellings were identical.

CHAPTER VII.

EXPLORATION IN THE SAN JUAN REGION.

IT is interesting and fascinating to read the history of the explorations of the Spaniards in Colorado, and trace on maps their routes in the mountainous country; yet it is doubtful if they penetrated into the heart of the San Juan Mountains. The best authorities seem to agree that Coronado did not even enter upon the present borders of southeastern Colorado in his famous march eastward. When Oñate entered New Mexico in 1591, he established a colony on the Chama. Thence adventurers penetrated farther to the north, exploring for gold and silver.[1] We learn of other explorations in the eighteenth century, when Cachupin was governor of New Mexico. The mineral wealth of the San Juan country

[1] Shafts of their ancient mines are found as far up as the Rio Hondo and Colorado in New Mexico, and even between the Culebra and Trinchera in Southern Colorado. — *Historical Sketches of New Mexico*, L. B. Prince (second edition, 1883), p. 164.

was the loadstone to attract these adventurers. Afterwards, in 1761, Juan María Rivera reached a point as far north as the Gunnison River.

In 1776 Escalante, accompanied by Don Joaquim Lain, who had been with Rivera, visited Colorado. He crossed the southwestern corner, journeying from Santa Fé through Abiquiu to Nieves, on the San Juan River. Some of the names which he gave have been retained to this day. [1]

The early history of New Mexico reads like a romance; but the existence of the primitive people, and the fact that the country contained archæological remains of great interest, seems to have been lost sight of till the middle of the present century, when exploring parties of the United States Government re-discovered, as it were, the homes of many of the pueblos.[2]

[1] The eastern section of the La Platte Range was called by Escalante "Sierra de La Grulla." — *Bancroft*, vol. xxx. p. 339. The La Plata River he called the San Joaquin, and in the cañon, says his narrative, were the mines sought for by Cachupin's explorers, and which gave the name to the mountains supposed to contain silver. — *Ibid.*, vol. xxv. p. 340.

[2] Notes of the Military Reconnoissance, etc., Lieut.-Col. W. H. Emory ; Journal of a Military Reconnoissance, 1846-47-48, Lieut. J. A. Simpson; J. W. Powell, "Scribner's Monthly," Jan., Feb., March, 1875 ; J. W. Powell, Official Report, Exploration of the Colorado River, Washington, 1875 ; J. Gregg, Commerce of the Prairies, New York, 1844.

The reports of these explorations so far as they refer to archæology deal principally with inhabited dwellings of stone and adobe. Lieutenant Simpson, however, discovered in Chaco Cañon deserted ruins of a people called Cliff-Dwellers, who are presumed to be the ancestors of the present Moquis and Zuñis.[1]

Mention has been made of early explorations, and of the routes taken by the Spaniards in Colorado; but it is doubtful if they went far enough west to meet any traces of the cliff-dwellings proper. Subsequent to the discoveries in New Mexico, we have no record of explorations of importance being made farther to the north, within the limits of Colorado, till the expedition of Capt. J. N. Macomb, in 1859. The published documents consist mainly of the report of Dr. J. S. Newberry, which was almost entirely confined to the geology of the country. Nevertheless, he visited many ruins of pueblos and cliff-dwellings; but unfortunately, though he made sketches and notes at the time, very little relating thereto has been published. He has kindly given me valuable information in regard

---

[1] Dr. Oscar Leow, in Report of the Chief of Engineers, 1875, gives the population of the pueblos at that time as eight thousand. See also discoveries by Lieutenants Whipple and Birnie, recorded in the same Report.

to some of the antiquities visited, especially those
on the San Juan River. This stream, which has
its source in Colorado, runs to the southwest into
New Mexico, and after making a great bend in
that territory, it flows in a more northerly direction, and cuts across the lower corner of Colorado
and Utah. Dr. Newberry found that from the
Cañon Largo in New Mexico to the junction of
the San Juan with the Colorado, the valley was
studded with ruins, few of which have ever been
described. They are either in open valleys or on
the cliffs and buttes, and it is evident that every
inch of the valley was once cultivated. It is also
probable that the inhabitants lived in fear of
attack from outside enemies, for some of the
buttes were crowned with defences. These de-
fensive works have with time almost entirely
disappeared.

In the printed Report cited above, Dr. Newberry
mentions ruins at Surouaro,[1] near the Dolores

[1] Surouaro is the name of a ruined town which once must
have contained a population of several thousands. The name is
said to be of Indian (Utah) origin, and to signify "desolation;"
and certainly no better name could have been selected. . . .
There is every evidence that a large population resided here for
many years, perhaps centuries, and that they deserted it several
years ago ; that they were Pueblo Indians, and hence peaceful,
industrious, and agricultural. — CAPT. J. N. MACOMB : *Report
of the Exploring Expedition, etc.,* 1859.

River, and also those on the Animas River and in Labyrinth Cañon. He also described a town of Los Cañones on the Rio Chama, in New Mexico. In regard to this, he has given me added information. The ruined town of Los Cañones is near Abiquiu Peak. It is situated on an isolated rock four hundred and fifty feet high, having abrupt and almost perpendicular sides, with an area on the top of about twenty acres. The town was entirely built of blocks of trachyte which were quarried at the bottom of the rock. Each stone was dressed on all sides, and must have been transported to the summit on the shoulders of the workmen. There are here large cisterns which have been excavated in the rock, with holes sunk for the reception of posts, which supported a superstructure, — doubtless to form a roof to collect rain-water. The wood-work around the cisterns and in the houses of the village has entirely disappeared by process of decay. When we consider that this wood-work was mainly cedar, which, in this climate, is almost imperishable, it will be seen that the town of Los Cañones has been abandoned for many years.

Later, explorations were made along the northern tributaries of the San Juan River, among and under the shadow of the great mountains that bear the same name. In these early days the San Juan Mountains were as wild and inaccessible as any mountain region in the West.

This great uplift is not a single range or series of ·mountain chains, but is composed of several clusters of great peaks. The northern portion, which is called the Uncompahgre Mountains, is formed by two groups which lie about Uncompahgre Peak and Mount Snaefell. Farther to the south are the mighty peaks which surround Silverton; and rising above Animas Cañon are the Needle Mountains. Still farther to the south lie the summits which go to make up the Conejos Range. Outlying groups, though properly considered as belonging to the San Juan system, are the San Miguel and the La Plata Mountains.

From Uncompahgre Peak in the north to Conejos Peaks in the south, both lying well within the system of the Sierra Mimbres, as the Spaniards called the mountains, is a distance of some seventy miles. From Telluride, on the west, to Antelope Park, on the east, is a breadth of forty miles. Within these limits are found peaks of granite, or quartzite, and of trachyte, — many-hued mountains [1] of every imaginable form,

---

[1] In Hayden's Report, 1874, F. M. Endlich, geologist, writes (p. 201) of the Rio Grande Pyramid : "Weathering

from graceful dome to tapering spire. There are beautiful mountain tarns and foaming torrents, deep, rugged cañons, and peaceful valleys. In among these several groups rise the Rio Grande del Norte, Animas, San Juan, Mancos, San Miguel, Dolores, Uncompahgre, and other important streams, all except the first mentioned being tributary to the Colorado River; for the Continental Divide, which enters Colorado at about 106° 50′ west longitude, reaches its most western point, 107° 35′, in the mountains east of Silverton, leaving most of the higher peaks of the San Juan ranges on the Pacific slope.

Until recently the valleys in among these peaks west of the Great Divide were very difficult of access. In fact, nothing is known of the connection of Americans with the heart of the San Juan Mountains and southwestern Colorado till 1860. In that year John Baker led a party of mining adventurers from Pueblo. They entered the country from the south from Tierra

with all the brilliancy that colors originated by ferric-oxygen compounds can produce, it presents, in its variety of shades as well as its elongated pyramidal form, one of the most striking features of the valley. But a short distance north-west of this mountain are the sources of the Rio Grande, which for more than ninety miles flows through one continuous area of volcanic country."

Amarilla, and went far up on the Rio de las Animas. This was a most difficult journey, for the Animas flows through a narrow cañon, the Needle Mountains rising above with precipitous walls.

Baker's Park, which has its name from the intrepid prospector,[1] is one of the most interesting valleys in this locality. It is as isolated as any mountain valley can be. Except by way of Animas Cañon, it can only be reached by crossing very high passes. Its elevation is 9,202 feet above sea-level.[2] To reach the summit of the several passes one must ascend from two thousand to three thousand feet. It was into this park that Baker and his companions were driven by Indians; some escaped, and others were killed.[3]

---

[1] Baker was a mountaineer of note. He had heard from the Navajos and other Indians that the royal metal existed in the mysterious upper regions of the Sierra Madre, proof of which was exhibited in ornaments and bullets of gold.—*H. H. Bancroft*, vol. xxv. p. 497.

[2] Denver & Rio Grande Railroad.

[3] Authorities differ. Rhoda states that Baker lost his life in the park in 1862 (Ann. Report U. S. Geol. & Geog. Survey, F. V. Hayden, Washington, 1876 ; Report on the Topography of the San Juan Country, by Franklin Rhoda, Assistant Topographer, pp. 465, 466). Bancroft states that '' Baker lived to be a wealthy cattle-owner, and to organize an expedition to explore the Grand Cañon of the Colorado. He was killed at the entrance to the cañon'' (vol. xxv.). From what I have been able to glean from frontiersmen, I am inclined to think the latter authority

The Report of the United States Geological and Geographical Survey of the Territories for 1874 is one of the most interesting of all the many valuable works issued by the Government press. Of especial interest to the mountaineer is that part of the volume which describes the San Juan Mountains.

In 1873 the Ute Indians released to the United States Government the right to all the land in the San Juan country which was supposed to be of value for mining purposes. It was the object of the San Juan division of the Survey to examine the region and determine the value of the lodes. This required considerable mountain-climbing.[1]

The party consisted of A. D. Wilson, topographer directing, F. Rhoda, his assistant, F. M. Endlich, geologist, and Mr. Gallup, barometric observer. The story of the adventures of the party is very interesting. If some of their narratives could be unearthed from their burial-place in the volumes of the Survey Report, — volumes which are out of print, and therefore inaccessible

correct, with the exception of the statement that he was a "wealthy cattle owner."

[1] Dr. Hayden wrote: "While Colorado has furnished so many districts of rugged mountain country, the one surveyed by this party during 1874 surpassed all."

to the general public, — and illustrated in a suitable manner, a book of surpassing interest could be made. They made the ascent of many peaks, most of them previously unascended, but were surprised to find a cairn on Rio Grande Pyramid, and thus to learn that some unknown climber had forestalled them. They met grislies and big-horns, and were caught in electrical storms which interfered with their work.

How changed all this is since those explorations! Then the country was very wild, though here and there in the parks and on the mountain sides were seen the picturesque cabins of the frontiersmen ; now the log-house is giving way to homely board structures, and the picturesque "wicky-ups" of the Utes and the cabins of the squatters are being succeeded by the unpoetical and commonplace product of the saw-mill. Such is notably the case at Silverton, the principal mining town in Baker's Park. Surrounded by a noble array of grand peaks, — Mount Kendall, King Solomon, Galena, Sultan, Bowlder, Bear, and other giants, — the village, itself the foreground of the picture, is made up of cheap and ordinary buildings.

In 1874–76, important archæological explorations were conducted, especially in Colorado, by members of Hayden's Survey.[1] Mr. William H. Holmes,[2] geologist of the San Juan division, examined many ruins in the valleys and upon the cliffs. Mr. W. H. Jackson, the skilful photographer of the Survey, made a very thorough search for architectural remains in Mancos, Mc-Elmo, Hovenweep, and Montezuma Cañons, and in the Chaco Cañon, in northern New Mexico, had the fortune to find a skull which belonged to the race of Cliff-Dwellers. The illustrations made from Mr. Jackson's admirable photographs attracted great attention to these marvellous ruins; but it must be remembered that the ground covered by these remains is extensive, embracing

[1] Hayden's Report for 1876, p. 383. Mr. Holmes's territory covered six thousand square miles (Hayden's Report for 1875). Dr. F. M. Endlich examined the ruins in the valley of the Rio de las Animas.

[2] Pottery of the Ancient Pueblos, by William H. Holmes, Washington, 1886, p. 315 : " In a number of ways the valley of the Rio San Juan possesses unusual interest to the antiquarian. Until within the latter half of the nineteenth century it remained wholly unknown. The early Spanish expeditions are not known to have penetrated its secluded precincts, and its cliff-houses, its ruined pueblos, and curious towers have been so long deserted that it is doubtful whether even a tradition of their occupation has been preserved, either by the nomadic tribes of the district or by the modern pueblos of the south. Certain it is that no foreign hand has influenced the art of this district, and no Spanish adventurer has left traces of his presence."

a section of several thousand square miles, and only a small area of so large a territory could be explored in three summers. In those early days, too, the travellers were exposed to all manner of hardships, were far from a base of supplies, and were at times in danger from hostile Indians. Thus it was with the region about Mancos Cañon, in which gorge many very interesting ruins were discovered, and which locality gives, perhaps, the finest examples of the remains of works of masonry in the West. The explorers had time only to enable them to pass through the main cañon, while recent developments have shown that the side gorges, or tributary cañons, contained by far the grandest ruins of the lost people.

I have endeavored, in these preliminary pages, to give the reader an account of explorations in the Southwest, and of some of the results already obtained. Though the country has been known and partially occupied for over three centuries, still there are large fields that have not been explored at all, and many sections would undoubtedly prove as interesting in the way of new developments as any yet investigated.

The following pages will present the story of wanderings in a limited district, where I have passed many very pleasant days among the mountains and cañons. There still remain multitudes of gorges and remote valleys almost entirely unknown, and the amateur explorer who shall essay to take part in future explorations will find much to employ and entertain him.

CHAPTER VIII.

THE SAN JUAN MOUNTAINS.

MY first entrance into the wonderland of the cliff-dwellings was effected by way of the towering mountains that form its northern bulwark. The spires of the San Juan ranges had exercised a powerful fascination upon me from the moment I first beheld them from far to the eastward, in scaling the savage arêtes of Sierra Blanca. The spell became more fixed when, after a year's interval, emerging from the cañon of the Gunnison, I saw their snowy summits piercing the blue sky only a score of miles to the southward. It was at its maximum as, leaving the main transcontinental line at Montrose, our little train sped directly toward them, giving us constant views, now, on the left, of the castellated ridges of mighty Uncompahgre, now, on the right, of the great peaks about Ouray, culminating in Mount Snaefell, whose form was barely traceable through the smoky haze that seemed to magnify its altitude. As at length we drew near the mining town that boasts the most remarkable site in the land, the early darkness of a September night had fallen, and we could see nothing of the grand scenery about us; but we knew that far above the glimmering lights which shone from the camps of the miners on the hillsides the great peaks were waiting.

We had several addresses to look up, as it was our first visit to Ouray [1] and we wished to obtain some information in regard to the mountains; but as name after name was read from our list, they were checked as sick or absent. The courteous proprietor of the Hotel Beaumont, however, on learning the purpose of our visit and that our bent was mountain-climbing, informed us that Dr. F. M. Endlich was stopping at that inn. I was delighted, knowing as I did of his excellent work as one of the geologists of Hayden's staff, and being sure that no man knew the country better. We were presented to him, very kindly received, and made still more joyful by being invited to ride with him high into the range the next day. The object of his journey was to start

---

[1] My friend Mr. Charles P. Howard was my companion on this and other excursions among the San Juan Mountains and the cañons to the south.

some delving operations at the Yankee Boy
mine.

The day following, we were off early, riding up
the Snaefell Toll road, through a magnificent cañon.
above a roaring brook. All along our morning's
ride were beautiful views of peaks and valleys.
The road is well built, and skirts the sides of the
mountains high up on their flanks. After riding
about two hours, the way turns to the right, and
high above us, blocking the end of the valley, we
saw Stony Peak, a beautiful diorite mountain:
we little dreamed that we should reach a point
beyond it that day. Its solid, rocky slopes give
it the appearance of a greater altitude than it
really attains. A half hour farther on we came
to a place under Potosi Peak where a log-house
had stood for six years, but was carried away by
an avalanche a year after its desertion. On the
sides of the mountains, a little below this point,
are grand exhibitions of havoc wrought by ava-
lanches. Earth-slides had ploughed a way
through great forests in broad, regular sweeps,
leaving the ground clean and bare of trees.

At 11.30 we reached a ranch, or mining camp
(Porter's), which is put down on the map as a
town.[1]   On the opposite side of the river is the

[1] Mount Sneffels.

entrance to a tunnel, which is eight feet high and
nine wide. It has already been extended thirteen hundred feet into the heart of the mountain;
it will strike the shaft of the Virginius mine at
a depth of nineteen hundred feet, and will be
considerably more than a mile in length. Now
the peaks on the left showed splendid towers
and sharp pinnacles. Dr. Endlich informed us
that the ridges had proved too jagged to allow of
a survey line to be run over their summits.

The wagon-road ends at Porter's, and burro and
mule trains do all the packing from this point up
and down from the "Yankee Boy," "Virginius,"
and other mines. They also are kept going all
the distance from Ouray.

At 11.45 we left the more travelled road which
leads to the Virginius mine, and followed a trail
leading to the "Yankee Boy." At noon we
passed the "Ruby Trust." Just below, in a little
valley where much grass grows, is a milk ranch.
The demand from the mining camps has called
such an industry into existence, and a dozen or
more cows pick a subsistence among the black-
willows which grow by the torrents. Passing
these pastoral groups, we left the tinkling of cow-
bells, and rode through interesting scenes. On
rock-beds by the trail were marks of glacial scor-

ing, and high above us on the peaks to the right
were splintered crags. One spire had a big hole
in it, through which the blue sky showed.

About noon we reached the " Yankee Boy "
camp, which consists of two very pretty log-cabins
near the stream. Here Dr. Endlich rested for a
short while, to direct the work of some miners
who were about to open a shaft. We were not
long delayed, however, but continued on and up.
In about an hour we reached timber line, and
at 1.15 the summit of Treasury Hill (elevation
12,125 feet), — a grassy alp from whose top is obtained splendid panoramic views of the encircling
snow-peaks. These snow-caps occupy nearly
300° of the horizon, and at the observer's back is
the dark wall of the Snaefell group. We spent
much time in taking photographs, securing sixteen pictures; six of these represent the panoramic view.

Treasury Hill is well suited for the location of
a mountain inn. It is easy of access, for a good
road could be built to the summit; there is
plenty of water to be found, for the turf is springy.
The region is very attractive. The many unnamed peaks are marked by a grace and beauty
all peculiar to themselves. But for one reason,
their charm to the mountaineer would be un-

equalled by any other range in the State ; but the
ever-present prospect-hole, found up to an elevation of thirteen thousand feet, gives the traveller
a feeling that he is not in a very wild country,
and that he has been preceded by many. The
appearance was so different from what I had met
with in other remote parts of the Colorado ranges
that I was struck with it on my first trip from
Ouray. This leads me to emphasize a statement
that I have often made before, — that wherever
minerals do not abound in the higher Rockies,
there, when away from trails, the traveller may
rest assured that few have been ahead of him,
and in many cases he may well feel that he is
a pioneer. But here, at the base of the final
cone of Mount Snaefell and the adjoining peaks,
we observed prospectors' openings, and stakes
marking claims were set in many places on the
grass slopes of Treasury Hill.

Looking to the south of Treasury Hill, one sees
a grand peak which towers up from a placid glacial lakelet. Sweeping down from near the summit come great ridges of sand and débris which
seem to show the path of an ancient glacier. The
lake is in a deep hollow, and is a wild spot. Rising above it on the west are the serrated ridges
of Snaefell. When the waters are calm these

pinnacles are mirrored in the lake, and the effect is beautiful,   One of the finest photographs which I ever obtained in the Rockies was secured at this place.

Leaving Treasury Hill at 3.15 P. M., we reached Ouray at dark, riding part of the way at a lively gait.   When the little town came into view, it was lighted up; and high on the mountain sides around, little glimmerings showed from the mining camps like answering beacons.

One result of our preliminary excursion was the making the acquaintance of a miner, a contractor and prospector of Ouray, who was at that time engaged by Dr. Endlich.   He had been up Mount Snaefell six years before.   He offered to go up this peak with us, and help carry our photographic apparatus.

The morning following we spent in climbing steep hillsides about Ouray.   This valley is in a hole, if ever any town was.   It is built on the bed of an ancient glacier above the terminal moraine. It is surrounded on all sides, save the narrow entrance to the north, by steep wooded slopes, which one must ascend but a short distance to catch sight of the noble peaks which lie back of them.

In the village we took pictures of burros and mule-trains, and on the hillsides views of log-houses and cabins. While among the hills, tremendous blasts were heard above us, and rocks came crashing down the slides, and fainter reports reverberated from the opposite mountain slopes. All day long in our ramblings we realized that the miner was at work in the mountains, and shaftholes were seen everywhere high up on the cliffs.

There are beautiful trees about Ouray; but the axe is already at work, and the town-folk must look out for the future, before it is too late to preserve the forests.

In the afternoon we rode on horses to Porter's camp. This place, as I have stated, is located on the map as a village. There is a store, over which is a loft in which are several beds; one of these was placed at our disposal. An addition to the building is used by the proprietor as a dwelling place. Next the store is a small house where meals are served to the mule-drivers and miners. Besides these is a large barn and a long, low building which is used for the storage of ores. This constitutes the town of "Sneffles Mount." The distance from Ouray by the road is seven miles; the elevation above sea-level is about 10,950 feet, or 3,310 feet above Ouray.

We enjoyed our stay at this mining camp, watching the mule and burro trains, and talking with the miners. A little way above the camp we were the observers of an approaching line of pack-mules, all loaded with ore from the Virginius mine. One of the animals took it into his head to cross the stream and wander among the scrub growth upon the opposite side. Several of his companions followed, and the driver, in endeavoring to "round them up," caused a general stampede, and, as a result, a couple of packs became loosened, and trouble was in store for the tired drivers. The burden of one mule revolved to a position under his belly, and naturally a furious spell of bucking and kicking resulted. It seemed as if that mule would destroy himself in his stupidity. He thrashed around till the ore was got rid of, and finally so entangled himself in the ropes, cinches, and saddle-gearing that he fell in the middle of the stream, and, lying on his back, continued to kick the air.

Later at the camp we were treated to an exhibition of horse-training. A cow-boy, who had left the joys of ranch life to spend his days in holes in the earth, undertook to mount and ride a bucking broncho that had hitherto kept all venturesome riders at a distance. A worse place could not have been selected in which to attempt to curb the spirit of such a beast. There was some commotion and excitement, at the start, while the horseman endeavored to get astride the steed; for he was driven back by the mustang, who let fly with hind legs, his heels making a sort of quiver and snap as they reached for the intended victim. Later efforts were more successful, and the trainer was soon firmly seated. The enraged animal snorted, plunged, and reared, but was unable to throw the rider, and in a fit of desperation took the bit between his teeth and dashed away. Open, clear space was limited, and in a blind manner the mustang mounted a pile of lumber, and then crossed a stack of logs, in among which we expected to see him break his legs and dash his rider among the timbers. Coming out of this difficulty in safety, he then took to the woods, where the cow-boy risked being struck off at every moment by the branches of the forest. He finally guided him into the road again, where horse and rider came down together in the dusty highway. Picking himself up, the broncho dashed off; but the cow-boy clung to the end of the rope, and was dragged through the stream, — a mountain torrent which ran near by. He held to the fiery steed, and the onlooking miners and mule drivers joining in, the combined weight of so many strong men checked the onward motion of the galloping horse, and he was brought to a stand-still. One of the miners now stepped forward, took off his coat and bound it around the head of the broncho, and after a little more fun the beast was cowed, and trotted up and down the road at the beck of his new master.

I had had some experience with bucking bronchos. Once in the Northern Rockies I used such a beast, — the kind that must be saddled and un-saddled with the greatest of care. One day, after a long ride, I dismounted, opened my camera box, which was strapped to the saddle, and carefully removed the instruments ; but the animal, look-ing around with his bad eye, saw the cover of the box projecting from his sides, and began a terrible dance. Levels, compass, diaphragms, barometer, tripod, and plates were distributed far and wide, so that we were able to follow the trail by the scattered remains. Dashing between two trees without considering the consequences, the broncho pursued his way. The box was knocked to pieces, and not until several searches had been made did we find the cover. Again, in another district, I rode an animal that in his plunges would land my nose on the soft place on the top of his head, between his ears, and would endeavor to throw me off at the brink of every precipice that we had occasion to pass; but in all my experience I never saw such a bucker as this one in the San Juan Mountains. During the evening, at the supper board, and in gathering knots of men after this meal was despatched, the conversation was about the cow-boy's feat, and his prowess was extolled on all sides.

So late in the season the mornings were dark and cold, so that we could not make very early starts. On this occasion we did not leave Porter's till 6.50. As on the day before, we passed interesting cabins and funny burros. Of the presence of one of these comical animals we knew nothing, except that two ears were sticking up over a ridge.

At the "Yankee Boy" camp we found our miner waiting for us. He followed us on foot, and we gained the summit of Treasury Hill at 8.30 o'clock. Here we fastened our horses to bowlders, divided our packs into three parcels, and made for a gully which leads up to a notch between Mount Snaefell and a peak to the east. In a few minutes we were on a great bowlder-field. On the opposite side of it we observed a couple of badgers among the rocks. Crossing the maze of huge blocks, we scrambled over a big moraine and descended into the trough. Above us loomed

the crags of a splendid arête. We left part of
our packs and some of our plate-holders at this
point, and started on our journey skyward. The
view began to grow more and more imposing, and
the ascent steeper. The savage arête fell below
us, and we could look over its spires to distant
ranges. At 10 30 o'clock we reached the notch,
and looked down, in a northeasterly direction,
upon a branch of the south fork of the Dallas
River. We rested for ten minutes at this point,
for which our barometer indicated an elevation
of 13,835 feet. Turning directly to the left, or
northwest, we entered a second gully, which was
about thirty feet wide. Steep walls rose above us
on both sides. We climbed in this narrow cañon
for thirty-five minutes, when we gained a second
notch, which was filled with snow. Carefully
climbing the cornice of ice, we obtained another
fine view into the Dallas valley.

Now some uncertainty entered into our work.
The miner tried to get up a gully by which he
thought he had ascended six years before; he did
not succeed. I tried another, which looked feasi-
ble, and after ten minutes' climbing reached a
ledge from which I saw an easy route to the summit. Our only trouble now was from loose rocks.
The whole summit seems to be falling to pieces;

great blocks rest on insecure foundations, and the slightest disturbance sends them bounding down the mountain side. I narrowly escaped a serious accident, by the giving away of what I supposed to be a firm rock, and a second and third clutch did but start other unstable stones to add to the clatter begun. A fourth grab, however, stopped my fall, and I came out with no other harm than a few scratches. At the present time, with no particular route laid out, there is just enough sharp climbing on the peak to make the ascent interesting; yet every side of the mountain appears to present the same difficulties. The first climbers seem to have had a hard time of it. Rhoda speaks of it as the "hardest climb of the season" (1874), and further states that "the first half of the height was very steep, but neither so tiresome nor so dangerous as the last half."

We reached the summit at 11.45 o'clock. The air was clear, though the smoke of forest fires in Montana, which a continued north wind had brought into Colorado, interfered with distant views to the north. The air was at rest during the one and three-quarter hours which we spent on the peak; it was also warm and comfortable.

After a short survey of the surrounding country, we took six pictures from the highest rocks.

The negatives, when developed, proved to be very good, and would have been much finer but for the lack of cloud effect and the hazy aspect of the sky. This fault followed us all through the San Juan Peaks, except about Silverton.

Snaefell has a good top, just enough space for one to move around easily and enjoy the view in all directions.   Before leaving Ouray we laid out on a cardboard compass bearings and distances of all important peaks lying within a hundred and twenty-five miles of our mountain, and thus we were able to identify many of the visible points.

Looking immediately down upon the north side, one sees a deep gulf, which is described by Lieutenant Rhoda in Hayden's Report. This recalls the manner of naming the peak. Dr. Endlich was standing in the abyss with one companion, who compared it to the great hole described by Jules Verne in his "Journey to the Centre of the Earth." Dr. Endlich agreed with him, and, pointing to the great peak above, exclaimed, "There's Snaefell." Thus the peak got its name, though it is pronounced by the people of the valley as "Sneffels," and it is so written on the maps and in the tables of the Coast Survey; wherefore it is part of the aim of this chapter to put on record the true designation, named after the Icelandic mountain Snaefell, lest ere long the grand summit be called "Sniffles." It is noticeable that already the inhabitants of the valley have a strong tendency toward this pronunciation.

Mount Snaefell is admirably placed for a view-point. On the north is the valley of the Dallas River, stretching far down to the mesa country about Montrose. To the west are Lone Cone, the San Miguel Mountains, Mount Wilson, Dolores, and Lizzard Peaks ; [1] to the east, the Uncompahgre group, with its marvellous castellated ridges, the main peak overtopping all ; [2] to the southeast, the peaks about Silverton ; back of these, the sharp points of the Needle Mountains; and far beyond, many peaks unrecognizable and unnamed. In the distance, south, we made out the La Plata Mountains, with Hesperis Peak, which dominates a valley which we hoped to know better in a few

[1] The San Miguel district is described as very picturesque ; Mount Wilson, the dominant peak, is one of the most massive in Colorado. East of this mountain is the remarkable trachyte obelisk called Lizzard's Head. The summit is 13,160 feet above the sea. From a noble pedestal the pinnacle rises 290 feet, with a diameter at the base of only about 60 feet : (Hayden's Report, 1874, F. M. Endlich, p. 207).

[2] The year following, I made an excursion to the summit of Uncompahgre Peak, and was thus enabled to view the remarkable scenery from a fine central view-point.

days. Yet we needed not look far to see the most
beautiful sights. Near to our station were peaks
unscaled and unnamed, which are marked by a
grace and beauty all peculiar to themselves, —
peaks with towers, peaks with spires, mountains
with graceful and beautiful forms. Down at our
feet, on the other side of the peak, were several
large lakelets, and we could see the upper edges of
the great snow-field on the north side of Mount
Snaefell, — the one that is seen so beautifully
from the Dallas River. It was a disappointment
that our time did not allow us to investigate this
ice-expanse, explore it, and make photographs in
detail, as no one has been near it, except, possibly, a few prospectors. Mr. Kedsie, the State
geologist of Colorado, told me, when we were in
Ouray, that he believed that this snow-field
might prove to be a miniature glacier. We observed one crevasse in an ice-stream miles away,
high up on another mountain to the west.

The north face of Snaefell is very ragged in
appearance, a number of jagged arêtes leading
from the summit. Notwithstanding our interest
in the perpetual snow-fields, one of the most
striking points of interest in the view was the
effect of the newly fallen snow ; white bands, as
ribbons, stretched across the face of lofty towers,

and in some cases reached for miles in parallel lines along whole mountain ranges, maintaining equal elevations. This is accounted for by the fact that the trachyte rocks lie in benches, these benches running across the face of the peaks, and the snow thus finds lodgment. Domes far and near were all pure white.

We left the summit at 1.25 P. M., stopping to take two views on the difficult ledges. Exploring for a new route, we struck a gully which was so filled with ice and loose stones that we were obliged to descend singly to avoid the danger from falling rocks. We hurried down the big gulch by which we had ascended, and gained the base of the arête, where we had left our plates, at 2.50 P. M. Here we took some more photographs; and reaching our horses at 3.45, arrived at the cabins at 4.15.

We had so much time at our disposal that we captured a number of pretty views around the log-cabins, and secured some of the negatives which serve as illustrations to this chapter.

One matter of interest to us in the view from the summit of our mighty peak was the fact that we could see, far away, fifty miles to the south, between the Dolores and Needle groups, the beautiful Hesperis Peak and the La Plata Moun-

tains, — ranges that stand over the valleys of the
Mancos, the Animas, and the Dolores Rivers,
whose banks are lined with ruins of a prehistoric
race, — scenes that we proposed to visit. Leaving
the San Juan Mountains with a regret which
would have been much deeper but that we were
bound for regions of varied interest, and knowing that we should be in sight of their tapering
crests for many days, we crossed the range and
descended through Animas Cañon to Durango.

CHAPTER IX.

MANCOS VALLEY.

THE Mancos River — Rio de los Mancos
(River of the Cripples ; though why it was
so called I have been unable to discover) — is
an alkaline stream which rises in the La Plata
Mountains. It flows through an open country
for some fifteen miles, then enters the cañon bearing its name, and soon after emerging from it flows
into the San Juan River, which in turn soon
unites with the great Rio Colorado of the West.

The valley of the Mancos is naturally approached from Durango, the principal town of
southwestern Colorado, upon the southern loop
of the Denver & Rio Grande Railroad, which
has its terminus at Silverton. The high-road to
Mancos leaves the valley of the Animas and passes
over an intervening plateau, or mesa, a distance
of some forty miles. The journey is an interesting one. The country, it is true, is in a general
way dry, but in fertile "draws" — as the local
usage calls the narrow valleys — are thrifty

7

ranches, and in some places crops of wheat and oats are raised without the aid of irrigation, while in other valleys are scattered groves of very tall pines. Dew here is almost unknown, and the rainfall is scanty; but in fierce winter storms snow sometimes falls even to the depth of thirty inches, disappearing almost as quickly as it came.

In two hours after leaving Durango the road to Mancos diverges to the north, while that which we have been travelling continues its course westward to Fort Lewis. Reaching the western edge of the mesa, the traveller looks down upon the valley of the Mancos. If he has made himself familiar with the reports of the survey parties, he will reach there expecting to see a parched and arid region, for the early explorers describe it as a desert. On the contrary, there lies spread out before him a beautiful land, where broad fields of golden grain cover hillside and valley. Near and far the prospect is grand and beautiful. Point Lookout, the great terrace-like tableland, or mesa, on the west side of the Mancos Cañon, springs like the abutment to a mighty bridge, the imposing Ute Peak rising beyond it in the west. Very beautiful in the distant background are the La Plata Mountains, which have been in sight during our ride over the mesa. Especially remarkable are the form and banding of Hesperis Peak, which declares its geological structure even at this distance of fifteen miles.

Mancos is an inviting place for its own sake, as well as for its being a point of departure for the archæological wonders of the neighboring cañons. Its history, like that of most Colorado settlements, is brief. In 1874 John Moss and six others came into the valley. They took up claims, but their golden interests lay nearer the mountains, or about Parrott City,—so called for the man by whom they had been sent out from San Francisco to prospect the country, which is not devoid of mineral wealth. There are placer mines on the high mesas to the north, while coal, on which the hopes of Durango rest, is found along the line of our way hither. The land where the village of Mancos stands was not "taken up" until more recent years, and as late as 1882 was traded away for a horse.

Near Mancos passed the old Spanish trail which led from Abiquiu in New Mexico to the Northwest. It is said to have been the route formerly taken by traders between Santa Fé and California.

This was the wonderland which my companion and myself, allured by more or less vague reports, were making the chief objective point of a visit to

southwestern Colorado; but even when we found
ourselves at Durango, it seemed difficult to obtain much information in regard to the now not
far distant Mancos country. In fact, if we had
not been well informed in regard to the literature
of the cliff-dwellings and ruined pueblos, we should
have been led to turn aside and visit ruins of minor
importance which exist in the lower valley of the
Animas, and which have already been fully described,— this upon the representation of enthu-
siastic residents of that valley. It was but by the
merest accident that we found ourselves instead
at the delightful ranch of the Wetherills, on the
banks of the Mancos.

Ranch-life is not without its fascinations, and
here one finds it in its most interesting form.
"Alamo Ranch," our place of sojourn, is an excellent type of its class, and a description of it may
serve for them all.

With the head of the house it is the same old
story as with many pioneers. Years ago, in poor
health and with little money, he rode a pony
across the plains from the Missouri River, and
took up a claim in this remote valley. With the
help of five strong, willing sons, all has prospered.
The soil, by irrigation, yields good crops, many
horses pasture near, and hundreds of cattle roam

the mesas. Everything about the Alamo Ranch
gives evidence of thrift and comfort. The barns
are large and well filled, and enormous stacks of
hay and straw are near the corral. A second corral — a very queer structure — was made by cutting off the tops of stunted cedars, and using the
trunks as they stood for posts. Poles were placed
on the top, and the whole then covered with straw.
The house itself, situated upon the terrace of an
ancient river-bed, is built of logs, strong and
compact. The dining-room — an important adjunct — is large, and has a generous fireplace.
Eight years ago not a tree stood near the ranch-
house; but now cottonwood-trees, that owe their
thrift to the water running in an irrigating channel through the yard and garden, give a grateful
shade. The whole neighboring scene is pastoral :
a picturesque home has been established in the
wilderness of sage-brush and piñon-pine. After
journeying though the more rugged portions of
Colorado, it is a place at which to stop and rest.

Stock-raising is the principal· interest, as the
great hay-stacks testify. In this valley the annual "round up" is still held, and will probably
be kept up for some years to come. Here one
may see the half-wild broncho trained and made
docile by plucky cow-boys. Here, too, we see

the breed of wool-bearing animals called Navajo sheep, with their shaggy fleece.

Bear and deer are plentiful about Mancos valley and on the mesas, especially when the heavy snows of winter drive them from the mountains. In December, 1889, the younger Wetherills killed seven deer, and were well supplied with venison. The annals of the hunters prove that comical things happen even in such an out-of-the-way place as Mancos. Near Webber Cañon lives a ranchman who owned a large dog, which one day brought a buck to bay. The deer was holding his own against the dog, and the frontiersman witnessed the fight from a distance. He had no gun with him, but determined to try and knock the buck in the head with a stone; but instead of accomplishing this, his intended victim sent him up a piñon-tree, and kept him there a long time.

The interest of the archæologist is excited immediately on his arrival. Near the Wetherills' ranch are some old ruins by the roadside. They appear like natural mounds, or heaps of stone; but close scrutiny refers their origin to human hands. Broken pottery is strewn all around, and specimens of many designs may easily be found. Much time would be required to determine the limits and size of the village or city, for it was of considerable extent. Tumbled-down walls cover a large field. Whether these structures were destroyed by an invader, or have simply crumbled of themselves, no one knows.

Such ruins are numerous in this region. The best specimens remaining are those at Aztec Springs, in the Montezuma Valley, the one next west of the Mancos. These are said to be the most extensive remains yet found in Colorado. Mr. William H. Holmes published in 1878 an account of his visit to them. According to his measurements, one of the structures is eighty feet wide, one hundred feet long, and, as then standing, twelve to fifteen feet high. The largest house measures one hundred and eighty feet in width, by two hundred feet in length. "The whole group covers an area of about 480,000 square feet, and has an average depth of from three to four feet. This would give in the vicinity of 1,500,000 solid feet of stone-work. The stone is chiefly of the fossiliferous limestone that outcrops along the base of the Mesa Verde, a mile or more away, and its transportation to this place was doubtless a toilsome work for a people so totally without facilities." [1]

[1] Hayden's Report for 1876, pp. 399 *et seq.*

There are ruins in other localities well worth investigation. West of Ute Mountain, near Yellow Jacket Cañon, is a building said to be twenty feet or more in height. It is built in a circle, within which is a second wall enclosing a circular room. The space between the two walls is cut into small chambers. In Montezuma Cañon there is an island formed by a parting of the creek, which is said to have been literally covered with arrow-points. Near here are many pottery kilns, and stone tools have been found. Most of the ruins in the western country, about McElmo, Yellow Jacket, and Montezuma Cañons, are lowland ruins, or remains of agricultural settlements. The cliff-dwellings are very small. These remains, as well as many others scattered over the broad plains and along Dolores,[1] Hovenweep, and other rivers, are not to be compared, as picturesque features, at least, with the ruins among the bold cliffs of the Mancos Cañons.

I have made reference in a previous chapter to the explorations of Holmes and Jackson among the Mancos ruins. Even until within a few years, the hostility of the Utes has rendered it dangerous for a white man to venture down the

[1] Escalante in 1776 saw ruins on the south side of the Dolores (Bancroft, vol. xxv.).

Mancos River without military escort, so it is not until very recently that much has been discovered to add to the important revelations of these earlier explorers. It was our fortune to meet at this ranch Richard and Alfred Wetherill, sons of our host, who are the owners of large herds of cattle, which roam through the valleys and over the mesas. Straying, as these often do, down into the land of the Utes, long rides are required to bring them back to the settlements. In taking these excursions, Richard, especially, has discovered many cliff-houses of great interest in Navajo, Moccasin, Acowitz, Cliff, and other side cañons in the Mesa Verde, and has given many of these abandoned dwellings a careful examination.

It was our good fortune to be the first to explore thoroughly this region with the Wetherills. In long trips with them we discovered ruins that had probably never been seen by white men before, and succeeded in scaling cliffs and entering dilapidated fortresses that appeared inaccessible. Equipped with a camera, we made many photographs and plans, and systematically explored the surrounding country. On this first trip we were accompanied by Richard and John Wetherill. Again, in September, 1890, I visited the country for the second time, and with Richard and Alfred Wetherill took a new route, and explored more southern cañons, journeying by Indian trails, parts of which had never been followed even by my intrepid companions. I take to myself, however, no credit of discovery, for one bent on finding hitherto unknown ruins in this locality must necessarily have one of the Wetherills along with him to inform him whether any supposed discovery is real or imaginary.

CHAPTER X.

UNDER the caption "Wild Tribes" I have made reference to the great tribe of Yutah Indians; but some description of these people as they exist to-day in the Land of the Cliff-Dwellers naturally forms a part of any description of this country. In the eastern section of their reservation, along the line of the Denver & Rio Grande Railroad, the Indians cultivate the land, and have taken some steps toward civilization; their farms are an interesting feature of the landscape as one sees them from the car windows. But farther to the west, in Mancos and McElmo Cañons, and about the Sierra el Late Mountains, the tribe known as the Weeminuches lead a roaming, pastoral life. They do not wish to be civilized; they tend their herds of cattle, their droves of horses and flocks of sheep, and hunt among the mountains, frequently trespassing beyond the boundaries of their reservation. They dwell in "wickyups,"—arbor-like shelters made of poles of aspen and covered with brush. These make good habitations for the summer months, but in winter, even when covered with skins, they cannot be very warm, and their occupants must suffer from cold; for snow at times lies deep on the plateaus, and fierce icy blasts from the San Juan Mountains sweep down through the cañons.

The Utes are decreasing in numbers, and will probably be removed ere long to lands to be set apart for them in Utah. Doubtless this change will be for the commercial interest of Durango and neighboring towns; but it will remove one of the picturesque attractions of the locality, and the ethnologist will lose the last chance to study the tribe in its native haunts.

Originally there were seven bands of the Utes. In northwestern Colorado were those of the White River country, whose chief was Nevava, — the story of their raids, ravages, and massacres are among the saddest annals of Indian warfare; south of these were the Uncompahgre Utes, led by Ouray, a chief who was very friendly to the whites. On the frontier of New Mexico were the southern Utes, under Ignacio, whose name is perpetuated by a town in the reservation. In Utah lived the Uintah Utes, and there were three bands in New Mexico.[1]

[1] Bancroft, vol. xxv. p. 470.

The Southern Utes, as now gathered in the reservation, are divided into three bands, — the Capotes, Muaches, and Weeminuches.[1] One band, whose chief is Mariana, camps south of Ute Mountain. The last chief of the Weeminuches was named Capazone. He died several years ago, and when we visited Mancos Cañon, his squaw was the ruler of the band.

These Indians often visit the Alamo Ranch, where we made our headquarters. They are made welcome, feel at home, and receive what they come for; namely, plenty to eat. They call the senior of the household their father. To this friendliness may be attributed the success of Richard Wetherill in making his discoveries and explorations in the cañons. It appears that what had been a hindrance to others had never deterred him from entering the wild regions. Even during the skirmishing warfare of only a few years ago, the friendly intercourse between the Wetherill family and the Indians was not broken, and they exchanged visits all through the period of the border fights. Yet recently the Utes have made way with at least one adventurer who had strolled into their domain.

[1] Bancroft gives Mowaches, Tabaquaches, and Weemiguaches as living in New Mexico. Other authorities write of Kapoti, Muachi, and Wiminuchi (vol. xxv. p. 470).

One evening during my stay, on returning from exploring some burial-mounds, I found three Utes at the ranch. They were to sleep in the hay-stacks, but had come to the house for supper. Two were from Mancos Cañon, and one was from the eastern section of the reservation, Los Piños. The latter spoke a little English, and had had some schooling at the agency; but this evening all hung their heads and were uncommunicative. We gave them some tobacco, which they rolled in paper and smoked. They were given a good supper, and then became more social. One was very fat, and his hunger was not easily satisfied. After the others had finished, he reached for the boiled bone which remained on the platter, and gnawed it clean. The blankets which they wore were of the ordinary government pattern, and not very showy. The Los Piños Indian and one of the Mancos tribe were without head covering, but the fat man wore a *sombrero ;* they wore buck-skin moccasins, the soles of raw-hide. On asking the Los Piños man if he made them, he answered that his squaw did the work, but that he could do it. The fat man's name was Wanamesa, and his comrade's Acowoitz, — a name very like that of one of his more prominent tribesmen. I found that the Los Piños Indian, who was the youngest of the three, could write a little, and after considerable talk he wrote his name in my note-book, — " Charvyz." After their supper they came into another room with me, and I talked with them for an hour. I showed them a volume of photographs, — views which I had taken, in their own country, of cañons, cliff-houses, and " wicky-ups." They recognized many of the pictures. Views of the mountains did not seem to mean much to them.

They saw my camera, which was standing in one corner of the room, and asked what it was for. On being informed, they denounced it as " no good," even Charvyz saying that it was " not very much good." Richard Wetherill, coming into the room, pointed the instrument at Aco-woitz, when he fled precipitately, and we did not see him again that night. We endeavored to persuade the remaining Indians to sit for their pictures the next day; only Charvyz consented. We succeeded, however, in getting pictures of all.

Interesting as we found this meeting with Indians at the ranch, it was still more so to see them in their homes. We afterward met them on the plateau and in the cañons. Our first meeting was in Mancos Cañon. Mr. Howard,

Richard and John Wetherill, and I had been exploring the Sandal Cliff-house, which will be described in the next chapter. We had left it, to journey farther to the south, following the stream. Soon the path abandoned the river, and by numerous obstacles was crowded high up on a terrace on the west side and above the trees, so that we obtained a clear view of the opposite walls and steep slopes. Suddenly we saw a drove of horses upon the hillside, and following them there rode an Indian, with a little Ute sitting behind him astride the steed. The red-man caught sight of our "outfit," and for a long time regarded us with a stern curiosity; he evidently considered us as intruders in his domain. He was a picturesque figure, without covering for his head, his black hair flowing down his back, and with a Navajo blanket over his shoulders. He did not take his eyes from us till we had passed down into the brush in the river-bottom.

The next morning found us *en route* for the portion of the mesa lying between Cliff and Navajo Cañons, this time to explore a western tributary of the Mancos. After an hour's riding to the south we came upon old Indian "wickyups," and in a few minutes more passed some which were comparatively new. Their owners were absent. These dwellings we photographed, for they were of great interest, as showing the difference between the abodes of the Utes, the present inhabitants of the valley of the Mancos, and those of the more skilful builders of the houses among the cliffs. The " wickyups " were made of poles of box-elder, thatched with twigs of willow and water-birch. An opening led right through them. These that we. photographed were for summer use, and especially for shade. The permanent abodes are covered with skins or tent-cloth. In one of these arbors we found willow-coil, which the Utes use for making water-jars, examples of which we saw later. Near by were mound-ruins. The valley is broad at this point, and there is considerable feed for stock.

Shortly we came upon a flock of sheep and goats ; and a little farther on, the barking and yelping of many curs warned us of our approach to an encampment. It was only that of one family, however, — the temporary home of Tabayo, the Indian whom we had seen tending his herd of horses the day before.

Two little girls fled from our presence into a " wickyup," of which there were three: two of these were covered with canvas. Old Tabayo came forth, not to greet, but to eye us with a surly indifference. He stood glaring, not moving a muscle nor relaxing his features. The young maidens now ventured out again, and began to throw stones at the dogs, which threatened to eat up our faithful canine companion. Richard dismounted, fearlessly advanced, and took Tabayo's hand, which the Indian seemed reluctant to grant. After a little broken and unsatisfactory attempt at conversation, our guide beckoned to me to come forward. I jumped from my horse, and was introduced with the utterance of the single word "Tabayo." The surly savage barely acknowledged my salute, but permitted us to look around. I should have felt more at ease if there had been fewer dogs at our heels. Tabayo exhibited a poor specimen of a stone axe from the mound ruins, which he was willing to barter for something. The only word he uttered was "Swap?"

A fire was smouldering in front of one of the wigwams, and the carcase of a sheep hung in a tree near by. We noticed in one lodge a water jar which was made from willow, stripped and made tight with piñon-gum. One of the two squaws came out and sat down. She was fat, and seemed of a jolly nature. She was occupied in mending one of Tabayo's moccasins: we had observed that one of his feet was minus a covering. He had lost one eye, and his name is said to have some relation to this fact. Richard asked him to allow us to photograph his group; but scowling, and lifting his stone axe to a threatening position, he made us understand by the use of this universal language, little assisted by his mother-tongue, that he would break the instrument if we undertook the operation. We might perhaps have secured a picture by strategy, although these Indians are as cunning as they are superstitious. We thought it best not to jeopardize our position, and run the risk of being driven from their territory and perhaps losing what negatives we had already secured of more valuable subjects. We offered him "un peso" for the desired privilege; but he rejected the offer with scorn. The Utes do not seem to care much for money. They would be more apt to plunder a stranger for his "outfit," saddle, or arms, than for any silver that he might carry.

Richard filled up Tabayo's tobacco-pouch, and we turned to ride away. Then the Indian seemed to relent, and fixed his price at "diez pesos;" but we did not heed him. I expected that he would call us back, but he did not. Richard said that he could have been brought to change his mind, if not for less money, for a reasonable share of our provisions, if we could have palavered with him for an hour; but we had no time to lose, and were already much belated.   Later on, I had no trouble in securing pictures of the Indians.   Tabayo himself has since had his portrait taken; but the operation required much time and considerable talk.   One picture has been sent to me which is said to have cost fifty pounds of flour.   The old Ute dressed himself in all his finery, consisting of beaded buckskin sash, and pockets of the same material.   He is now a sufferer from rheumatism, and it is to be hoped that he does not charge it to the fact that his features have been impressed on a gelatine film.

Leaving these children of the wilderness, we rode on down the valley, and after an hour's journey turned up a rocky path to climb the mesa. Far down the cañon, — which here was of wide expanse and very level, — we spied the smoke of a larger Indian encampment.   Suddenly a mounted redskin emerged from the group of "wickyups," and galloped furiously over the plain.   As we mounted higher, he put spurs to his horse, and soon overtook us.   With only a glance at those of us who were behind, he rode up to Richard and took his proffered hand; yet there was mischief in his look as he demanded our intentions. Our guide pointed out the direction of our journey, — over the mesa, and home by a western route, — and added to his sign language the words "one sleep." The Ute observed our spade; he seemed dissatisfied. Then he expostulated in Ute, Spanish, and English, so mixed up in vocabulary that it was difficult to comprehend; but out of the jargon I caught the following ideas: "White man rich; Indian poor. White man dig up Moquis, make Ute sick: little Ute, big Ute, all heap sick."[1] He made motions indicative of the process of excavation, and with a threatening, superstitious look seemed bound to prevent any such sacrilege of the graves of the departed tribes. Richard insisted that we did not intend to disturb the bones of the Moquis, but were to photograph the ruins. This latter operation he explained by pointing to our apparatus, and going through the motions of looking through glass. Wap (for such was his name) now made a demand for toll for the privilege of going over the mesa; but Richard, pointing to the high climbing sun, answered, "Ken savvy" (*Quien sabe*). As

---

[1] This reference to the Moquis shows that the Utes have a tradition that the Moquis are the descendants of the Cliff-Dwellers.

we turned away, Wap exclaimed: "No money, Richard no come back in cañon." The Ute stood motionless, regarding us till we were high among the upper cliffs of the cañon, when he turned wrathfully away and galloped to the north toward Tabayo's "wickyups." I must confess that I watched these tents till they were all out of sight, for I feared to see Wap and Tabayo mount their ponies and gallop down toward the lower encampment, where generally a dozen or more braves are to be found. Such a force, if gathered, could have compelled us to return to Mancos, thus frustrating the important plan of our expedition. We were not even armed, to show bluster if threatened; a rickety revolver in Richard's belt being the only weapon in the outfit.

Taking into consideration his friendship for Richard, Wap's conduct was very strange. Two days before, John Wetherill and others had met him, and offered him four dollars to guide them over the mesa by the route which we were following, — a way known only to Richard and the Indians. He did not catch the idea, accompanied them only a little distance, and then demanded his money. This was refused him, — which may explain his surliness. Wap is not a man of any

influence, and Richard said that he did not antici-
pate any difficulty from that source. The next
winter Wap changed his tactics, and was of great
assistance to the explorers of the cañons, though
at first he was inclined to hinder their work. A
person of more brains and greater influence in the
valley is Acowitz. He is a friend of Richard's,
and we hoped to meet him on the mesa, where he
frequently herds his cattle in company with some
of the Navajo Indians; but he did not chance our
way. He was somewhat in Wetherill's debt for
the loan of a rifle and other small favors.

CHAPTER XI.

MANCOS CAÑON.

MANCOS CAÑON is the great median vein passing through the Mesa Verde, which receives from right and left the numerous tributary cañons. The distance from Wetherill's Ranch to its southern opening in the San Juan valley is estimated at thirty-seven miles, and the width of the cañon at that place is about three miles. In the narrower portions, the gorge is perhaps half a mile wide. At the opening to the north, the mesa walls, like great portals, are separated about five miles with a sloping, nearly level, tract between. The whole length of this cañon is of interest to the archæologist, but so much of it has been described by Messrs. Holmes and Jackson that it remains only to call attention to a few ruins that chanced to escape their observation.

Two hours' journey from Mancos brings one to the mouth of Webber Cañon, the first tributary gorge on the left, or southeastern, side. All the ranches have been passed before this point is

reached. The path is henceforth an Indian trail,
and the river must often be forded. Here, however, it is only worthy the name of creek, for the
irrigating ditches of the farmers above take the
greater part of its waters. Lower down, however,
it regains some of the loss. Scarcity of water is
the scourge of the country. Mancos River is an
alkaline stream. The springs, rarely found, are
alkaline; but when much rain falls, the potable
quality of the river water is improved.

Near the junction with Webber Cañon are
numerous mounds similar to those near Mancos
village. Their presence is first intimated by
fragments of pottery scattered over the ground.
The building material was sandstone. Excavation shows regular walls, and in the burial-mounds
bones of the ancient people are found.

An hour and a half farther to the south there
is a very interesting cliff-house, which is situated high above on the right, or northwestern,
cliff. It takes but ten minutes to reach it from
the trail below. The ruins are placed under an
arched cliff, the space of which we estimated at
thirty feet high in front, and about eighteen feet
in the rear, where the masonry abuts against the
stone roof of the cave. Six front rooms are still
to be seen, only three of which are well pre-

served. Two of them are circular. All the space
under the cliff, perhaps a hundred feet in length,
had evidently at one time been covered by the
structure.[1] The material used in the building
was sandstone, of the same composition as the
surrounding cliffs. The stones of the walls of the
house gave evidence of having been rudely faced.
The mortar used was evidently made from the
fine alkaline detritus of the cliffs. Some of the
walls had been plastered with material taken
from the river-bed; it was put on with the hands,
and the finger-marks show the manner of doing
the work. In the north enclosure is a painting
of a small sized hand in red. On one of the walls
is a human figure five inches and three-quarters
high, represented playing a flute-like instrument.[2]

The floors of the room are pretty well demol-
ished. From the north apartment a peculiar
shaped door leads into a back chamber. But for
the fact that it is the entrance to an enclosure
which could have had no light, one would be

[1] While I was making notes, my companion made a ground-
plan, which I am able to present here. The measurements were
obtained by pacing off the different rooms. The walls, generally
twelve inches thick, are sixteen inches thick in a circular house;
the plan so represents it.

[2] A flute was found in a cliff-house, and is now in a collection at
Denver.

inclined to take it for a window. The lintel is a charred cedar stick ; there is a good stone sill. From the number of sandals found in this building, it is called the Sandal Cliff-house.

The house fronts the east. Upon the opposite side of the cañon, quite low down, is one building, and high up on the cliff is another; they are both small, and difficult to detect with the naked eye. It has been stated for a fact heretofore that all the houses were built upon the western sides of the cañons, so that the rising sun could shine into them. This is an error, for some of the finest ruins have been discovered upon the eastern face of the cliffs.[1]

The night following our first visit we pitched camp a few miles south of the Sandal Cliff-house, in a clump of box-elders at a point a little above the entrance to Cliff Cañon, a tributary of the Mancos from the west. By reason of a heavy shower which had drenched us, the branches were so wet that we could not cut any boughs for a bed ; so, stretching a wagon canvas, which had covered one of the packs, between two trees to keep off the rain, we spread blankets on the

---

[1] Crest of the Continent, p. 160 ; also Hayden's Report, 1876 (W. H. Jackson), p. 376 : "We could not find even the faintest vestige of ruins or houses upon the eastern side."

ground, and then dried ourselves by the camp-fire. During the evening I was able to make notes by the firelight. We also changed our exposed negatives from their plate-holders, in order to be able to start in the morning with thirty-two dry plates in readiness for use. The river ran very near our camp. The liquid was disagreeable to the taste, and very muddy. We bailed some from a pool that contained water that had overflowed from the stream, and thus had had time to settle. The disagreeable flavor is not noticeable in coffee, but merely boiling the water does not seem to improve it. The night was pitch-dark, and we could see nothing when beyond the immediate reflection of our camp-fire. Rain continued through the early part of the evening.

Near this natural camping spot are picturesque views of cliffs and ruins. To see to advantage one of the best of these, which is perched high up on the western side and which is difficult to detect without a glass, we found it necessary to climb the eastern wall of the cañon to a height of about two hundred feet. From here the ruin seems quite inaccessible, but may be reached without much difficulty. The cañon walls from this outlook are very bold and striking; upon the opposite wall, coal shows in seams. A most interesting feature of the views was a grand tower standing at the entrance to Box Cañon, a short gorge to which this name has been given, though all the very short cañons bear the generic name of "box cañons," because they end abruptly against high cliffs, thus differing from the long, lateral gorges, which are likely to offer easy entrance from their upper extremities. In this particular cleft there are a number of small houses which have never been in any way explored. Our camp, in the trees below, veiled with the ascending smoke, was very picturesque.

A few miles south of our camp we found other ruins in the valley; they are some distance from the river, on the western side, at a point where the cañon widens. It is doubtful if they have ever been described. Within a short distance of each other, two towers are standing, similar to the watch-towers of the early explorers. The ruin of the higher one measures twelve feet above the ground. The smaller one is six feet high, and twelve feet in diameter. There are ruins near the latter, which are thirty-six feet in diameter. This building does not show great skill in workmanship, as the stones of the walls do not break joints.

Ruins to the south of these towers, both upon

the cliff and in the valley, have been visited and already described ; for this reason, and especially because we had laid plans to ascend the mesa and investigate more promising localities in the side cañons, we did not take the time to examine them.

CHAPTER XII.

ACOWITZ CAÑON.

ACOWITZ CAÑON, which joins the Mancos
from the east, is one of the finest of all
the side ramifications, and contains antiquities
well worth investigation by the archæologist. A
good Indian trail traverses the whole length of
Mancos Cañon, and similar paths lead for some
distance up its branches; but to visit the remoter
ruins it is much easier to ascend the walls of the
main cañon to the surface of the mesa, ride across
the plateau, and thus strike the tributaries well
up toward their beginnings: such was our method
of approach in the visit, the story of which I am
about to tell.

Our temporary home was a camp in Mancos
Cañon, the situation of which was described in the
last chapter. My companions were Mr. Howard
and Richard and John Wetherill. Our outfit
consisted of five horses and one pack-mule. One
of the horses, called Kaiser, is a splendid pack-
horse, requires no leading, and finds his own trail.

The mule Jiffy also served us well; but one night, though hobbled, he strayed far away, and we saw him no more. He probably joined Tabayo's herd. This straying of animals is one of the annoyances of camp life, and an extra man is useful if for no other purpose than to " round them up " in the early morning, for they often roam a long way from camp in their search for food.

It was early on one glorious September morning that we four left camp, mounted upon our several animals, to ascend to the top of the steep mesa on the east, journeying by a rough Indian trail, bound for some ruins in Acowitz Cañon. Near the trail a sharp ridge, or dike, of igneous rock has been thrust up through the sandstone. In twenty minutes we were forced to dismount and lead our horses the rest of the way; and as much more time spent in hard walking brought us to the flat summit of the mesa, perhaps eighteen hundred feet above the river. From this point is obtained a good view of houses in Cliff and Mancos Cañons, also an outlook toward the western mountains, — the Sierra El Late. An hour's ride across the country, over a comparatively level tract, through piñon-pine and junipers, brought us to a fork of Acowitz Cañon in which are certain remarkable ruins.

We tied our horses to trees at some distance from the great ravine. Here, as on the edge of many of the other chasms, there is no soil, grass, or trees within several hundred feet of the brink. The surface is smooth sandstone, with here and there great hollows filled with rain-water. These places are called "tanks" by the ranchmen, and are the only sources of water supply for deer or cattle on the mesa.

To be exact, the group of ruins which we proposed to photograph is situated on the western cliff of the third left-hand fork of Acowitz Cañon. As one skirts the edge of the abyss the structures below are invisible, neither is there any way of descending to them; so we worked our way around the head of the gorge to the opposite, or eastern, side, and there found a wall which must have been used as a fortification. Originally the breastwork was built with great care, for the stones are regular in shape, and have been cut and faced. But few of them remain as placed by the builders; yet this little rampart gives a clew to the explorer who is hunting for a way down into the cañon. Stepping over the tumbled-down walls and looking over the precipice, we found hewn steps on the face of the cliff, and descending by them, as members of the tribes must have done,

— as perhaps their ferocious adversaries may have
done also, — we soon reached the bottom of the
gorge, and hurriedly scrambled up to the interesting ruins.

A strange, wild, lonely cañon. No sounds were
heard to disturb the scene but the croaking of
ravens as they flew over our heads. Perhaps
they were welcoming us as old friends.[1] The
great arched cliff hangs high above the ruins; but
a little way from it the cañon ends in sheer solid
walls which sweep around in a curve. Looking
all about, we see but one exit above, and that by
the steps which we had descended. Perched in a
little cleft over our heads was a second group of
buildings, apparently inaccessible and in good
repair. I suggested that we try to scale the cliff.
Richard thought it impossible, and pointed to the
trunk of a tree that leaned against the ledge,
which he had placed there, and which failed by
some six feet to reach the rounding sandstone
terrace above. While our companions were rum-
maging around the lower rooms, John and I tried
our luck in squirming up the tree. It was of no

[1] American Antiquarian and Oriental Journal, vol. x.,
March, 1888, No. 2 : "The Raven in the Mythology of Northwestern America," by James Deans: "Ask any of the Indians
'who made the world and all things therein,' and the answer
will be, 'The raven.'"

use; we could not reach far enough, and there was not the slightest hold or crevice for the fingers. We got an old beam from the ruined floors, which was a trifle longer than the log, and fastening a rope to one end, we placed the timber up against the cliff by the side of the other stick. With the aid of the rope, we could gain the top of the timber with less expenditure of force. We made several attempts in vain to gain the ledge, each time being obliged to come down to rest; but at last my companion, whose arms and legs were of long reach, after removing much dust and debris, was able to get a hand-hold, and clambered up. I followed him, and calling to our friends, they sent up the spade and camera, then mounted after us, and we entered the mysterious rooms.

How long since human foot had trod those sandstone floors? Surely not since the forgotten prehistoric race had deserted the caves. Certainly no white man had ever entered these walls before, and the superstitious Ute would not dare to venture under the shadow of the cliff. After our difficult tussle in scaling the wall, we thought we might be rewarded by finding some rare specimen of the ceramic art known to the dwellers among the caves, — a graceful pitcher, or a water jar, standing on a shelf waiting to be called for; but, on the contrary, there was an air of desolation around the vacant quarters. All was cleaner than the ruin below; it showed no signs of being a burial-place or ground in which it would be profitable to dig. Undoubtedly the best places for such examination are in the lower ruins.

But we found the little home of a bygone people unique and interesting. We now made some photographs of the strange structures. The outer walls had been built upon the edge of the ledge, and to investigate the different rooms we were obliged to bend or crawl behind them, for the cliff was very low in the rear. In one of the rooms we dug a little, but found nothing. The door to this room is of peculiar shape, being wider at the bottom than at the top; we could see no reason for it. The floor of the ledge was covered with fine dust; when disturbed by the spade it raised a choking cloud, and forced the would-be excavator to beat a retreat. On the south corner is a very curious little building to which there is one entrance. This, again, one would take for a window, but that no light could pass through it when the whole wall was standing. The race of Cliff-Dwellers were not liberal of space when they built their doors; we did not find one high enough to pass through without bending. It was

a fascinatingly queer place; but we must away,
for time-consuming caution must be used in the
retreat from our citadel. We were struck with
the strength of the position, and believed that we
could have kept in check a small army of primitive combatants, if they should have dared to
storm our position, armed, like ourselves, only
with stones.

The rope made our descent comparatively easy.
My friend and Richard went down first; then we
lowered the plates and camera, threw the spade
after them, and I followed. John, as the last
man, looped the rope around a pile of masonry
and let himself down. He reached out and got
hold of the tree in safety; but by a little sliding
of the cord a big rock was dislodged, and in falling it crashed upon the package of dry-plates, and
I have two pictures fewer to show than would
otherwise have been the case.

We now set to work to explore and photograph
the lower structure. For the latter work we
were well equipped. We had three lenses, — a
Dallmeyer of eleven inches focal length, one of
nine inches, and one of four and one half inches.
The Dallmeyer was used for all distant views, and
as often as possible to prevent any distortion; but
even the lens of shortest focus had often to be

brought in play when in among the ruins and for taking interior views. Many parts of the structure were in a good state of preservation; sticks and supports were still intact. Floors were made of sills of cedar, willow sticks were then laid over, and the whole was covered with plaster. In most cases the floors have fallen in. We noticed some peculiar arrangements: one such was a sort of low cubby-hole, outside of the main structure, which was eight feet front and five feet deep, with two little doors. This may have been used as a store-room. We found much broken pottery, — fragments of large bowls which it would be possible partially to restore.

One very remarkable thing, which showed the eccentricity of the builders, was a room which appeared to have no entrance. In fact, I walked around it once without discovering that I had passed a room. A little investigation revealed an entrance from the top. The enclosure was eight feet square, the entrance a hole seventeen and a half inches aperture. The ceiling, of wood, was plastered over, and was very firm. Any photographers who may be looking for a dark room in which to change plates at mid-day when in this locality will find this room as good a place as could be desired. From its top I took a photo-

graph of one end of the edifice, as it was a good
view-point. We took advantage of this position
to photograph some interesting grooves on a ledge
of smooth sandstone which is at the base of the
walls. This was accomplished by placing the
camera flat on the roof of the enclosed room, and
letting the lens hang over. These grooves in the
rock were made by the natives in sharpening their
tools; most of them were large, and probably used
for grinding axe-edges. On another ledge we
observed smaller ones, where awls, knives, and
needles were whetted.

One of the central rooms is well plastered,
smooth as a modern wall. A round room had
piers below the ground floor. These piers also
are plastered. In the sides of the walls were
little recesses which may have been used as
shelves. There is also a door similar to the one
that we saw and photographed in Mancos Cañon.
Above this door the walls are hollow.

We had not the time at our disposal to excavate
among the rubbish, but the slightest investigation
showed that the place was rich in relics. A little
scraping away of the earth revealed human bones,
cloths, matting, etc. From this cliff-house the
Wetherills and their companions have obtained
many specimens.

In walking among these ruins one passes over tumbled-down walls and crosses remnants of shaky floors of charred cedar. My companion noticed fossil shell impressions on a stone which had been used in the building.

Early in the afternoon Mr. Howard and John Wetherill returned to camp, while Richard and I started off on a tour of investigation. We discovered some houses in the fourth left-hand fork of Acowitz Cañon, a place that had never been visited before. Here stands a good circular room with two doors. On the sandstone plateau, near the brink of the gorge, is the most remarkable crevasse that I ever saw. I called Richard's attention to it, and I hope he will show it to those who may travel with him in future. In a land where erosion has played such a part in modelling the face of the country, a crack is phenomenal. Unfortunately, I made no measurements, and cannot give a reliable description; but it was more than a hundred feet long, and about a foot in width. It was inclined at a considerable angle, and the bottom could not be seen. It would be an awful place to fall into, as man or animal would be wedged in, and assistance could not avail. It made me shudder to look into it, though standing on the edge of a high cliff would produce no such sensations.

From this box-cañon we went far up on the main gulch, leaving our horses behind. From a pocket of the cañon we had remarkable views down the whole length of Acowitz to the Mancos, and then through that depression to the magnificent mesa which stands above the river's place of exit. It was a truly sublime sight. I photographed the view, but the camera fails to show the beauties of the distant lines. The nearer scene is a wild one : quaking aspens grow in the upper part of the gorge, and in the bottom are tall, stately pines which climb to the height of the top walls, and were even with our eyes as we looked across the cañon.

I lost, from a stupid double-exposure, several very interesting negatives of a weird ruin, almost inaccessible, which occupies a secluded cavern in this cañon. One single picture, however, which is left to me, shows the remarkable structure of the cliffs, and the beautiful curve which they make as they sweep around to the east. What a dark and gloomy place did these mysterious people select for their home, or fortress, whichever name we may give to it! A stronghold surely it was, impregnable to a foe armed only with arrows and clubs. The great cliff spanning over it shielded the inhabitants from all attack from the tableland above them; and the vertical cliffs below could not be scaled when rocks were being hurled from battlement and tower above.

As the sun was already sinking in the west, we could not examine closer this remote structure, but hurried back to our horses, and reached our quarters long after dark.

CHAPTER XIII.

CLIFF CAÑON.

NARROW winding defiles, precipitous walls, bold headlands, and overhanging ledges are the characteristics of Cliff Cañon, and within its labyrinths are most remarkable ruins. Here it was that Richard Wetherill found a large structure, which he has called the "Cliff-palace."[1] This ruin, which is situated in a branch of the left hand fork, can be reached in about five hours from Mancos Cañon. A long day's ride over the mesa from the ranches will also accomplish the distance ; but the journey from the Mancos is by far the easier of the two.

On reaching the brink of the cañon opposite the wonderful structure, the observer cannot but be astonished at the first sight of the long line of solid masonry which he beholds across the chasm, here but a thousand feet wide. In the first

---

[1] Cliff Cañon was visited some years ago by a prospector named Osborn, who, however, did not penetrate far into the heart of the mesa. He is to be credited with the discovery of a ruin called the " Brown-stone front " (Montezuma Journal [Cortez], Jan. 26, 1889).

burst of enthusiasm it strikes one as being the
ruins of a great palace erected by some powerful
chieftain of the lost people. The best time to see
the ruin is in the afternoon, when the sun is
shining into the cavern. The effect is much finer
than when viewed in the morning. Surely its
discoverer did not exaggerate the beauty and
magnitude of this strange ruin. It occupies a
great space under a grand oval cliff, appearing
like a ruined fortress, with ramparts, bastions,
and dismantled towers. The stones in front have
broken away; but behind them rise the walls of
a second story, and in the rear of these, in under
the dark cavern, stands the third tier of masonry.
Still farther back in the gloomy recess, little
houses rest on upper ledges. A short distance
down the cañon are cosey buildings perched in
utterly inaccessible nooks. The scenery is marvellous; the view down the cañon to the Mancos
alone is worth the journey to see.

To reach the ruin, one must descend into the
cañon from the opposite side. What would otherwise be a hazardous proceeding is rendered easy
by using the steps which were cut in the wall by
the builders of the fortress. There are fifteen of
these scooped-out hollows in the rock, which cover
perhaps half of the distance down the precipice.

At that point the cliff has probably fallen away; but, luckily for the purpose of the adventurer, a dead tree leans against the wall, and descending into its branches, he can reach the base of the parapet. One wonders at the good preservation of these hand-holes in the rocks; even small cuttings, to give place for a finger, are sometimes placed exactly right even in awkward places. It is evident why they were so placed, and that they have not been changed by the forces of the air in the several hundred years that have probably elapsed since they were chipped out by an axe made of firmer rock. There occurs to my mind but one explanation of this preservation: erosion by wind is one of the important factors in chiselling rock forms about the Mancos, and as we observed sand in these hollows, we suppose the wind at times keeps the grains eddying round, and thus the erosion in the depression keeps pace, perhaps even gains, on the rate of denudation of the smooth cliffs.

It takes but a few minutes to cross the cañon bed. In the bottom is a secondary gulch, which requires care in descending. We hung a rope or lasso over some steep smooth ledges, and let ourselves down by it. We left it hanging there, and used it to ascend by on our return.

Nearer approach increases the interest in the marvel. From the south end of the ruin which is first attained, trees hide the northern walls; yet the view is beautiful. The space covered by the building is four hundred and twenty-five feet long, eighty feet high in front, and eighty feet deep in the centre. One hundred and twenty-four rooms have been traced out on the ground floor. So many walls have fallen that it is difficult to reconstruct the building in imagination; but the photographs show that there must have been several stories; thus a thousand persons may easily have lived within its confines. There are towers and circular rooms, square and rectangular enclosures, all with a seeming symmetry, though in some places the walls look as if they had been put up as additions in later periods. One of the towers is barrel-shaped; others are true cylinders. The diameter of one circular room, or estufa, is sixteen feet and six inches; there are six piers in it, which are well plastered, and five recess-holes, which appear as if constructed for shelves. In several rooms are good fireplaces.[1]

[1] Fireplaces have been rarely observed among the cliff-dwellings; Mr. Holmes writes of one in Mancos Cañon (Hayden's Report, 1878; see illustration, plate xxxiii. fig. 6). Dr. Fewkes describes fireplaces in ruins near Zuñi: "There is a great similarity in the internal arrangement of

One of our party built a fire in the largest one, which had a flue, but found the draught too strong, for his light wood came near going up with the smoke. In another room, where the outer walls have fallen away, an attempt was made at ornamentation: a broad band had been painted across the wall, and above it is a peculiar decoration which is shown in one of the illustrations. The lines were similar to embellishment on the pottery which we found. In one place corn-cobs are imbedded in the plaster in the walls, showing that the cob is as old as that portion of the dwelling. The cobs, as well as ker-

the several chambers which have been excavated. We often find in one corner a square flue resembling a chimney, which may or may not be open below on the floor of the room. These flues are made of small stones, and are covered with mud on the interior. In one room there were two of these flue-like structures, which were placed side by side. From the small size of the rooms and the absence of evidences of smoke in these flues, one is reluctant to admit that fires were extensively used in these chambers. Still, in some there is good evidence of fire. In the Chaco ruins, according to F. T. Bickford ('Century Magazine,' October, 1890), 'neither fireplaces nor flues are to be found, and it is probable that fires were never built in the living apartments.' While this may be true of the Chaco ruins, which are similar to those of the Zuñi reservation, it is certainly not true of all the rooms in Hesh-o-ta-uthla. More research is necessary to settle this point." (A Journal of American Ethnology and Archæology, edited by J. Walter Fewkes, p. 108 ; Houghton, Mifflin & Co., Boston, 1891).

nels of corn which we found, are of small size, similar to what the Ute squaws raise now without irrigation. Besides corn, it is known that the race of Cliff-Dwellers raised beans and squash; we frequently picked up stems of the latter. It is not known that they owned domestic animals, but they had turkeys.[1] We found a large stone mortar, which may have been used to grind the corn. Broken pottery was everywhere, similar to specimens which we had collected in among the valley ruins, convincing us of the identity of the builders of the two classes of houses; and we found parts of skulls and bones, fragments of weapons, and pieces of cloth. One nearly complete skeleton lies on a wall, waiting for some future antiquarian. The burial-place of the clan was down under the rear of the cave.

Notwithstanding the imposing name which we have given it, and which its striking appearance seems to justify, it was a communistic dwelling. There is no hall leading through it, and no signs that it was a home prepared for a ruler of the people. It owes its beauty principally to the remains of two towers; it probably owes its magnitude to the fact that the length of the platform and depth and height of the natural

[1] The pueblos had sheep after the coming of the Spaniards.

arch allowed of such a building in such a remote quarter.[1]

Naturally this huge ruin interested us as much as anything that we met with in our trips. It deserves study by expert archæologists. Thorough and careful excavation would perhaps reveal many relics which might throw light on the early history of the primitive inhabitants. It is to be hoped, however, that any work which may be done here in the future will be carried on under competent supervision, and that the walls will not be damaged in any way. Collectors, so far, have been very thoughtful. With a suitable appropriation, this structure could be so arranged that it could be converted into a museum, and be filled with relics of the lost people, and become one of the attractions of southern Colorado.

---

[1] This large open cave, as well as others that I have described, are natural, and do not appear to have been enlarged in any way by man. Lower down on the Mancos River are small caves which have been deepened and the entrances walled up.

CHAPTER XIV.

NAVAJO CAÑON.

NAVAJO CAÑON is a tributary of Mancos Cañon from the northwest. It joins, near the southern extremity (there being but one branch south of it), a much smaller one, called Ute Cañon. With three great branches of its own, Navajo Cañon much exceeds the Mancos itself in the number of miles of cliff-front.[1] The different arms are of about the same size, and unite into one near the Mancos. Ruins are found — over a hundred in all — in these three nearly parallel gorges and in many short box-cañons which extend out on all sides. Many of these remains of the cliff-dwelling people are unimportant. They are either very small, or have for the most part crumbled away. Others are well preserved, and appear as if only very recently deserted. Such a one exists, perched high up on a cliff that looks, when seen from the bed of the cañon, as if newly constructed. Timbers project through the high

---

[1] I hardly dare to estimate the number of miles, but it must be over a hundred.

walls, but there is no opening below them. One of my comrades gained an entrance by splicing poles together, and climbing up to the top of the walls. He found in the interior ten whole pieces of pottery in plain sight. The inhabitants used coal for fuel.

In another cañon are three interesting ruins in close proximity on the same side of the gorge. The primitive families might have been very neighborly if they had chosen to be. In one of these houses is a fireplace which has a raised hearth and fender; this was built of stones, and plastered. In one of the other houses, in an estufa, or circular room, is a fireplace which was once honored with a chimney; some of the work remains. These ruins can be reached from the mesa by descending through a cleft in the rocks. It is not a difficult feat to perform, except when one is burdened with a heavy pack.

Perhaps the best-preserved remains of a cliff-dwelling eyrie — at least one that retains more features of interest than many of the other ruins — is one that is situated in a right-hand branch of the second large right-hand fork of Navajo Cañon.[1] It is about three hundred feet long. Under a natural sheltering rock, remains are

[1] This is applicable to one going up the course of the cañon.

standing of three stories. Originally the building was probably five stories high, and was built in the form of a terrace, the two lower tiers having been built outside the limits of the arch, and lower than the platform of the cave, so that what we now see standing are the three upper stories. The lower parts of the edifice, more exposed to weathering, have mostly crumbled away. The entrance to apartments in the cave was probably made by passing over the top of the outside buildings.

In one portion of the ruin, at the base of the doors to the upper rooms, are many timbers which project out from the wall. Though the floor of the scaffolding has all fallen away, this would seem to show that there was once a balcony here.

The masonry of the building is all of very good order; the stones were laid in mortar, and the plastering carefully put on, though, as the centuries have elapsed, it has peeled off in certain spots. At the north end of the ruin is a specimen of masonry not to be seen in any other cliff-house yet discovered. This is a plastered stone pier which supports the walls of an upper loft. It is ten inches square, and about four feet high. Resting on it are spruce timbers which run from an

outer wall across the pier to the back of the cave.
Above the pier is a good specimen of a T-shaped
door, with lintel of wood and sill of stone.[1]

One lintel was made with eleven small sticks
about three quarters of an inch in diameter, which
were very smoothly plastered over. The floors
were also made in the same manner, by placing
twigs and mud over the sills. Lying among the
débris are masses of plaster which show the
grooves made by the sticks and twigs, and many
fragments of mortar still hold the sticks imbedded in them. Sills and beams were neatly
smoothed on the upper surfaces.

Much care was used in finishing the walls; little holes were filled up with small stones or
chinked with pieces of broken pottery, of both
painted and indented ware. Some of the walls
are decorated with lines similar to those described
as existing in the cliff-palace. Other designs are
somewhat different. One of more interest is a
rude picture which represents two turkeys fight-
ing. Below one opening we found the door that
originally closed it. This door was a thin stone
slab fourteen and a half inches wide at one end,

---

[1] I have described piers as existing in some estufas, but they
are built into the main walls. This pier is detached, and stands
by itself.

and fifteen and a half inches wide at the other end, and two feet and one inch high. It had an average thickness of an inch. Imbedded in the walls, upon each side of the opening, were staples made from loops of willow. Lying at the base of the entrance was the stick which had held the door in place. We put both in their proper positions, and the result shows in the accompanying illustration. There were several of these slabs lying among the mass of stones.

In one room is a fireplace; but as there was no chimney, the walls were blackened by the smoke.

On the outer edge of the ruin, beyond the protection of the overhanging cliff, is a spruce-tree which has grown from the centre of a room whose walls have fallen. This tree is about eighty feet high, and, measured at a point twenty inches from the ground, it is three feet and three inches in diameter. Judging from the rate of growth of forests in moister climates, we presume that this tree must be at least two hundred years old, and we have here one slight clew as to the shortest limit of time that must be put on the interval passed since its desertion by its occupants or their extermination. The building must have been vacated, then the walls given time to crumble and

fall away, before the seed could have taken root.
How long a time this occupied, probably no one
will ever know. To obtain an approximate knowledge of the age of the tree, one of the same size
could be cut from the cañon near by, and the
rings of growth be counted. To cut this particular tree, would be to destroy a picturesque adjunct
to the ruin, and to obliterate a monument to its
age.[1]

In describing some other ruins, I must say
that I cannot locate them exactly on the map.
Our approach to them was from a camp in the
bed of one of the main branches; but we travelled
so far through seemingly interminable ravines,
and crossed so many gorges, that we lost track of
their number.

At the end of a box-cañon is one of the grandest natural arches in the region. On the ledge
under this arch was once a great building; but as
the cave is very damp, most of the structure has
fallen. The stones and remains of pottery and
implements have been disintegrated, and little
remains that is of special interest. One remarkable feature, however, deserves mention, — a great
stairway leading down to the ruin. But for this,
the investigator would be obliged to make a

[1] See illustration facing p. 156.

long détour, and follow the cañon bed for some distance. There are eighty of these stone steps. Some are natural, others were cut in the ledges, while more are stone slabs simply fitted into place. The descent is thus made with ease.

There is another mighty arch in one of the Navajo cañons which shelters a ruin well worthy of description. This building is visible from the brink of the cañon, as one journeys up its length. To find a place to descend, one must round the head of the cañon, and follow a long winding route over and under ledges to the cañon· bed. The noble arch rises a hundred feet above the natural platform. The sloping bed of the cañon reaches to the base of this platform, which rises like a terrace to a height of about twenty feet. Trees and bushes grow up to the base of the ledge. The ledge is approximately four hundred and eighty feet long, as we determined by pacing. This is the largest cliff-dwelling yet discovered in this region. The front walls were built upon the rim of the platform, which is curved to the general form of the amphitheatre, and gives the building the appearance of an impregnable fortress. The walls, of solid masonry, remain firm, and present an imposing front. In the centre the stones have broken away in such a manner as to leave standing a high wall, which gives a gothic appearance to the ruin.

At one end three stories remain standing; the upper room is squeezed in under the arch, and was entered by a low door. These high-standing walls show how the cliff-dwellings were originally constructed. They reached to the roof of the cave, and were necessarily higher in front than in the rear, for the cliffs make over them an arch which served as a natural roof.

As first built, much more space than the platform was utilized, and a lower terrace occupied. Walls that divided rooms and formed the ends of the structure run down among the trees and bushes; the lateral walls have all fallen down. In some places, where the ground is steeply inclined, the stones of the ruin lie like talus on a mountain side.

On ledges above the main edifice are smaller buildings, and in one cranny is a long, low structure with thirteen loop-holes in front and two at the end. Those in front open at different angles, so that any approach from below could be observed by the watching cliff-climbers.[1]

This ruin, if undisturbed, will doubtless remain

[1] From this fact I have named this ruin the "Loop-hole Fortress." Occasionally it is referred to here as the "Crenellated Fortress."

for centuries in about its present condition, and
cannot but fascinate the archæologists who shall
chance to visit it. Perhaps these same ruins, if
placed on a plain or in a quiet valley, would not
appeal so strongly to our sense of the marvellous;
here, in a remote cañon, far from the river, far
from water of any kind, with high frowning walls
upon three sides, and an untracked ravine below
it, one wonders why the lost tribes should have
selected such a place for their home.

The standing masonry in itself is of interest.
The solid front does not give the idea of patch-
work, as presented in many of the buildings of the
Cliff-Dwellers. Standing on the parapet and looking along the front line, there is not a break to be
seen in its continuity, except as the platform
bulges in or out. Save that the stones were already at hand, shapen by the elements, as they
had broken off from the cliffs and overhanging
ledges, the marvel would be greater that a people
with only stone and wooden tools could have accomplished such a work.

The light of noonday floods the walls of the
ramparts, and penetrates into the deep recesses
of the cave; but, as the sun sinks westward, a
dark shadow creeps across the front of the cavern,
and the interior is in deep gloom. It is then that

the explorer, standing among the crumbled walls
and gazing up at the loop-holes above, or following with his eye the course of the cañon down to
its end where it joins the greater gorge, wonders
what events happened to cause this strong fortress
to be deserted or overthrown. There must have
been a fearful struggle between a people who
were emerging from barbarism, and more savage
hordes, or some great catastrophe of Nature over-
whelmed them.

CHAPTER XV.

ARCHÆOLOGICAL NOTES.

OUR first vacation drew to a close, and we soon took our way eastward, passing through San Luis Park, then under Sierra Blanca and over Veta Pass to the plains. A heavy fall of snow, and on-coming cold nights, deterred us from attacking the peaks of the Sangre de Cristo range, and we turned our backs on the Rockies for a year. Yet the memory of great peaks and archæological wonders went with us, and the latter were kept constantly before us by reminders from the old comrades, who sent us many relics which they found in their continued explorations and excavations in the wondrous cañons. These relics were of especial value to us, for during our expeditions the time was principally consumed in photographing the ruins for picturesque features and also in detail; we had but little time to dig. It was in the interval that elapsed between our two trips that the Wetherills made their systematic excavations, though previous to this they had collected valuable material, which now rests in the rooms of the Historical Society of Colorado at Denver.

The story of the inception of this work is as follows: One day Richard was riding on the Mesa Verde, looking for some strayed cattle. As was his custom, he scanned all the little side cañons in the fascinating search for vestiges of ancient people as he passed along the brink of the precipices. He discovered some remarkable ruins in a locality which he had never chanced to visit before. Returning to the ranch, he met a party of hunters, — among whom was Mr. Charles McLoyd, of Durango, — whom he succeeded in interesting in his discovery to such an extent that several of them spent some three months in excavating among the different ruins. Besides the numerous nearly perfect specimens of jars, bowls, needles, baskets, cloth, matting, etc., eighteen skulls were found, — all articles of great interest to the student of ethnology and archæology.

Hitherto, excepting a few relics found by Richard Wetherill, only broken pottery or inferior articles had been picked up from cliff-dwellings, and but one skull had been discovered, — that found in Chaco Cañon, to which I have already referred.[1]

[1] The title of the catalogue of the collection reads as follows: "Catalogue of Ancient Aztec Relics from Mancos Cañon,

Not till early winter did these enthusiasts undertake systematic exploration for a second and more complete collection. As the months wore on, it grew larger and larger, and of incalculable value to the student of archæology. But it was secured under difficulties. It took ten pack-animals to do the winter's work ; yet they all came out in better condition than when the enterprise was begun. This is surprising when we realize the difficulties of transportation. On one trip the snow was belly-deep to the horses and mules. The corrugated jars, swung in sacks, were "packed out" on the shoulders of the explorers, — a difficult task, considering the distance from camp, in a branch of Navajo Cañon, southwest of the "Cliff-palace," and forty-five miles from the ranch.

Up to March 14, 1890, they had examined in all one hundred and eighty-two houses, but few of

La Plata Co., Southwestern Colorado, collected by an Exploring Party consisting of Charles McLoyd, L. C. Patrick, J. H. Graham, A. Wetherill, during the winter of 1888–89." In this list A. Wetherill represents his several brothers also.

In 1890 a very large collection of relics was obtained by Charles McLoyd and C. C. Graham. These relics were found on the lower San Juan, principally in the Grand Gulch Cañon in Utah. The collection is now in the possession of Rev. C. H. Green (Bulletin of the American Geographical Society, vol. xxiii., Dec. 31, 1891 ; The Cliff-Dwellings of the Mesa Verde, by W. R. Birdsall, M. D. This is a very valuable and interesting account of Dr. Birdsall's visit to the region in 1891).

which yielded much in the way of relics. They
visited one hundred and six houses in Navajo
Cañon alone, and worked two hundred and fifty
miles of cliff-front. Most of the ruins in Navajo
Cañon were of large size, containing from thirty
to one hundred rooms each. Many ruins were
found in unsuspected places; many were worth a
visit just to look at. One was found which had a
good spring in the back part. Some appeared comparatively new; others as if they had been long
occupied; and still others were much dilapidated,
scarcely a vestige remaining, except small pieces
of pottery, which age does not seem to affect.
They commenced their excavations in the first
cliff-house in Mancos Cañon, — that described in
the fifth chapter, and illustrated in chapter xi.[1]
They began at a point thirty-five feet to the left
of the figure seated on the wall in this illustration.
It will be observed that the ground does not run
off very steep; yet there is sufficient slope for the
débris thrown over to slide down the hill, and
thus easily to be got out of the way. Notwithstanding the difficulties and disagreeable nature
of the work, — for the alkali dust is choking,[2] —

---

[1] Phototype, " Sandal Cliff-house," facing p. 120.

[2] Signs of alkali are represented in some of the illustrations.
On that facing p. 125 the vertical lines and the character like a

they followed up the digging, and were very successful; they discovered one hundred sandals, —
some in good condition, others old and worn out,
— a string of beads, a pitcher full of squash-seeds,
and a jug with yucca strings passing through the
handles. This jug was filled with corn well shelled,
with the exception of two ears.[1] They unearthed
a perfect skeleton, with even some of the toe-nails
remaining; it had been buried with care in a
grave two and one half feet wide, six feet long, and
twenty inches deep. A stone wall was upon one
side, and the bottom of the grave was finished
with smooth clay. The body lay with the head
to the south, and face to the west. It was
wrapped in feather cloth, and then laid in matting.
Buried with it was a broken jar, a very small un-
burned cup, a piece of string made from hair, and
one wooden needle.

Next to the wall mentioned above was found
the body of an infant, which was dried and well
preserved like a mummy. It was wrapped in
thin cloth, over that was feather cloth, and encas-
ing all was willow matting tied securely with
yucca strings.

figure 5 are the result of alkaline efflorescence. The same pheno-
menon is noticeable in the cave in the illustration facing p. 143.

[1] I have in my collection a corn-cob with twelve kernels remaining in it. There were originally forty-one kernels in one
row.

They found also a piece of rope five eighths of an inch in diameter, with forty-eight strands, bone needles, awls, stone axes with and without handles, twine, arrow-points, a bow-string, a large jar, coiled ware, and four skulls.

In one ruin were found several skeletons, which showed by their condition that the dwellers in that house had met with a violent death. In a room which had but one entrance, and that from the top, four persons had been killed, — probably with stone axes, for their skulls were broken in. They had probably been surprised, and attempted to escape by the chimney. One man's legs were in the chimney, his trunk in the fireplace, and his head and arms in the room. Across one arm lay the body of a young person, with head broken in the same way, and over both was thrown a mat.

In one house was exhumed the body of a woman. To enter this house they were obliged to splice poles and climb up much as we did in entering the upper ruin in Acowitz Cañon. The appearance of this skeleton was somewhat different from other specimens found; one circumstance noted was auburn hair, though it was turning to gray: they also found a large bunch of red hair. In another house the excavators found a piece of string in a bowl. I have examined this string

11

under a microscope, and, comparing with sample plates, find it to be made of cotton. This fact shows that the Cliff-Dwellers had intercourse with the pueblo tribes of New Mexico and Arizona, where cotton was raised.

The excavators also found some long wooden sword-shaped sticks, as to the purpose of which they were at first in doubt; since, they have decided that these were used to beat yucca in order to separate the fibres, of which they found quantities. Another discovery was a bowl of walnuts, — a nut which does not grow in Colorado. The bowl was found in a room at a depth of three feet, yet it was on an upper floor that had fallen in.[1]

Of over one hundred pieces of pottery found,

---

[1] Through Mr. Cosmos Mindeleff, of the Bureau of Ethnology, Mr. Fernew, Chief of the Forestry Division of the Agricultural Department, has kindly given the following information: "The walnut which you left for inspection can be hardly anything else than *Juglans rupestris,* corresponding with specimens of the fruit on hand. The field of distribution I have noted on the enclosed map, as far as known. You will notice that it remains below the plateau country."

According to the map furnished by Mr. Fernew, *Juglans rupestris* is found in southwestern Texas, southern New Mexico, southeastern Arizona, and along the coast of California, between San Francisco and Los Angeles. The nearest approach of the tree to Mancos Cañon is about two hundred and fifty miles. This fact also leads one to believe that the Cliff-Dwellers perhaps traded with the Indians of the south. The walnuts were not perforated, so were probably not used as ornaments.

no two are alike. It was anticipated that many duplicates of bowls and mugs would be found; but all were in different patterns of painted design.[1] The indented or coiled ware was evidently the kind which was most in use, more so than the painted vessels. Some were buried near the doors, with their rims even with the surface of the ground, and were probably used to collect water. Certain jars were blackened by soot, and were probably used for cooking purposes.

From a study of some of the relics of pottery found, it appears that the Cliff-Dwellers imitated certain features of their architecture in the products of the kiln. One specimen, a mug, in my collection illustrates this point: in the handle a

---

[1] Of more than a hundred fragments of painted and indented ware which I picked up, all are of different design. One indented piece was painted on the interior surface. These are not common.

Referring to the San Juan district, Mr. Holmes writes: "The ceramic remains are more uniform in character and apparently more archaic in decoration than those of any other district. They belong almost exclusively to two varieties, the coiled ware and the white ware with black figures. . . .

"It is unfortunate that so few entire vessels of the painted pottery have been found in this region. The fragments, however, are very plentiful, and by proper study of these a great deal can be done to restore the various forms of vessels" (Pottery of the Ancient Pueblos, W. H. Holmes, Washington, 1886, p. 315). This lack has now been remedied by the finding of many beautiful and complete specimens of painted ware.

hole has been cut which copies the shape of the peculiar doorways seen in this region.

One day I was occupied photographing a ruin in Navajo Cañon. My companions were busy with pick and spade, each intent on his own work. One called, "See this specimen of pottery; is n't it a rare one?" I looked, and observed what he held up to my gaze. It was a fragment of fired ware about three inches square, with numbers of fine lines above a broader band. I had found a number of specimens of similar kinds; but not wishing to throw cold water on my companion's enthusiasm, I answered, "Very good." He responded, "You don't seem to think much of it;" and he turned the piece over, that I might see the other side, or exterior, of the piece of bowl or jar, where I observed a picture of a bird which we suppose was intended to represent a turkey. The head was gone, having been broken off, and we searched for the missing piece in vain among the débris; but, notwithstanding its incompleteness, it was a good find, for such specimens are rare. I have already called attention to similar painting on a wall in a Navajo Cañon cliff-house,[1] and again I have seen a fragment of a bowl on which was a drawing representing two turkeys possibly about to commence a fight.

[1] See p. 149, chapter xiv.

As for clothing, it is probable that wearing apparel was scarce. It may have consisted of feather or cotton blankets, hair leggings, and sandals, strings of beads on their arms, around their necks, and over their breasts, with perhaps a buckskin cap upon their heads, adorned with plumes of turkey feathers. Buckskin may have been used as material for making blankets instead of fibrous stuffs. Numerous pieces were found, but none of sufficient size to give a clear idea of the use to which it was put.

It was thought at one time that certain articles of fabric were made from wool; but inspection with a microscope has proved that the material was milk-weed fibre. It is unlikely that sheep were in the country, except the native bighorn, whose horns are found in the cañons and on the plateau.

In a work of this kind it would be hardly of interest to give a schedule of relics found, or to describe them in detail, — such description would only interest the specialist;[1] but a few of the more important relics deserve mention.

---

[1] I have already referred to the work of W. H. Holmes, "Pottery of the Ancient Pueblos." This excellent monograph, published in the Fourth Annual Report of the Bureau of Ethnology, contains much information in regard to the pottery of the tribes who once inhabited the valleys of the San Juan and its tributaries.

Sandals were made from fibres, woven, for the most part, in a simple manner by crossing the strips. They were fastened to the feet by strands of the same material. They were made very compact, though light shows through them. The strands are about three sixteenths of an inch in width, and one sixteenth in thickness. The plaits are half an inch wide and very thin. As an exception, one sandal in my collection is woven of much finer material, and looks like an old cloth slipper. When it is held to the light, one cannot see through it. It has a neat pattern woven in it, similar in design to markings on pottery.

The only specimen of modelling is a small image that looks more like a bear than anything else. Several pipes have been found, and quantities of stone axes, and a few bows and arrows. With a large skeleton in Acowitz Cañon was found a bow which was four feet eight and one half inches long; the string was of sinew.

The Cliff-Dwellers used hampers in which to carry burdens, and straps to put through the handles of their ollas, or water-jars. They had brushes made of fibres.

Interesting as are the relics in themselves, it is upon the antiquity of the cliff-dwellings that one is led to speculate while among the ruins. It is

a question difficult to decide, or to give any
opinion upon. Located in a dry climate, protected from all aërial forces, I see no reason why,
if unmolested, the walls should not stand a thousand years as we now see them, and, in my judg-
ment, there is no reason to doubt that they have
stood a complete cycle.[1]

The valley ruins have gone a long way farther
toward complete destruction than have the cliff-
dwellings. This has led one authority to suggest
that the cliff-houses "owe their construction to
events that immediately preceded the expulsion
of the pueblo tribes from this district." The
same authority also states that "the final aban-
donment of the cliff and cave dwellings occurred
at a comparatively recent date, — certainly subsequent to the Spanish conquest."[2]   But allow-

[1] Hayden's Report, 1876, W. H. Holmes, p. 386. Mr.
Holmes, in writing of standing stones found on the Dolores
River, says: "That the placing of these stones occurred at a
very early date is attested by the growth of the forest, which is
at least three or four hundred years old. In a number of cases
the stones are deeply imbedded in the sides and roots of the
trees."

[2] Hayden's Report, 1876, W. H. Holmes, p. 408. This statement is undoubtedly true of cave and cliff dwellings farther to
the south. It is stated that even some of the Spanish monks
dwelt at times in the cliff-lodges. For an account of comparatively recently deserted pueblos, see "Journal of American
Ethnology and Archæology," vol. i., "A Reconnoissance of
Ruins in or near the Zuñi Reservation," by J. Walter Fewkes.

ing that the cliff-houses were deserted only three hundred years ago, this would not help us to assign a date for the building of some of the larger structures, which, from what we know of the tools employed, must have been the work of time. Not a scrap or piece of metal has been found in the débris which rest upon and among the tumbled-down walls. Many of the stones that we see, which were employed in the rearing of the great edifices, must have been laboriously shaped by an almost shapeless stone axe. Such work, carried on under so great difficulties, did not allow of villages being constructed in a day.

One fact which has been investigated by that eminent archæologist, Mr. A. F. Bandelier, would seem to throw some light upon the subject: "It does not appear that the Sedentary Indians of New Mexico ever made, within traditional and documentary times, any other than the painted pottery in greater or less degree of perfection."[1] This would prove that the specimens of indented ware which we have found cannot be less than four hundred years old: how old the painted pottery is, we know not.

[1] "Report on the Ruins of the Pueblo of Pecos," published in the "Papers of the Archæological Institute of America," p. 105.

As for the state of civilization of the ancient people, it could not have been far advanced. A community who could huddle together in such small, close, unventilated quarters, who buried their dead under their floors and under the rear of cliffs and back of their mightiest houses, could not have reached a very high ideal of refinement. Yet it may be we judge too hastily. Perchance these remote fortresses were subjected to a long siege by crafty Ute or fiery Apache, wherein the heroic defenders stood out to the last; and as man after man fell at his post, his body was perhaps hastily imbedded in débris at the rear.

As for the builders, who were they? Where did they come from? These are difficult questions to answer. Mr. Justin Winsor, in the "Narrative and Critical History of America," writes in regard to the early investigators in the field of the prehistoric lore of America, "Few . . . in discussing the problem could say, 'I have ventured to inquire,' without presuming to decide."

Recognizing the pertinency of these words, and realizing that the discussion of such topics belongs to those who have made a survey of the whole broad field with knowledge of all the facts, both archæological and linguistic, I disclaim all desire to put forth a theory as to the origin and disappearance of the Cliff-Dwellers. If my work may claim any merit, it will be due to the fact that the future antiquary may learn from the reproduction of my photographs, and their description, the condition of the Mancos ruins in the years 1889 and 1890; while, therefore, I would not venture to theorize from the small collection of facts which we have obtained, I may be permitted to call attention to a few generally conceded facts of history. From the seventh to the twelfth century, the Toltecs invaded Mexico from the north; following them came the Aztecs. It is possible that Colorado and New Mexico may have been the former dwelling-place of these migratory nations; or if they came from the northwest, straggling bands may have strolled into the lands we are describing. Yet all connection between the people of the North and those of Mexico had probably been lost long before 1530 A. D. It is not even probable that either knew of the existence of the other, though a belief has been current that those people worshipped Montezuma. Again I must quote Mr. Bandelier : —

" What the Indians themselves say of this tale, I have not as yet ascertained; but the people of the val-

ley all assert that the people of the pueblo believe in it;
that they even affirmed that Montezuma was born at
Pecos; that he wore golden shoes, and left for Mexico,
where, for the sake of these valuable brogans, he was
ruthlessly slaughtered. They further say that when
he left Pecos he commanded that the holy fire should
be kept burning till his return; in testimony whereof
the sacred embers were kept aglow till 1840, and then
transferred to Jemez.

"There is one serious point in the whole story,
and that is the illustration how an evident mixture
of a name with the Christian faith in a personal re-
deemer, and dim recollections of Coronado's presence
and promise to return, could finally take the form of
a mythological personage. In this respect, for the
study of mythology in general, it is of great importance. That the sacred fire had originally nothing
at all to do with the Montezuma legend, is amply
proven by the earliest reports.

"It will also become interesting to ascertain in
the future how many pueblos, and which, concede to
Pecos the honor of being the birthplace of that famed
individual, and how many, as is the case with other
great folks in more civilized communities, claim
the same honor for themselves.

"I cannot, therefore, attach to the Montezuma
tale any historical importance whatever, not even a
traditional value." [1]

[1] Report on the Ruins of the Pueblo of Pecos, p. 112, in
"Papers of the Archæological Institute of America," Boston,
1883.

It is interesting to note what Mr. Bandelier writes in another work, of a tradition met with at Mitla, two hundred miles south of the city of Mexico: —

"I found there among the Indians the singular tradition that the buildings of Sansuanch — as the ruins are called east of the Venta Salada, at the foot of the Sierra de Zongolica — had been the former home of Montezuma, from which he had started to conquer Mexico. The parallelism with similar traditions among the Pueblo Indians of New Mexico, far to the north, is indeed remarkable."

It has been customary in popular writings to claim for the Cliff-Dwellers that they were a different stock even from the Pueblo Indians; some going so far as to state that they were a white race. There is no ground whatever for any such conclusion. As a rule, they had black hair, and were probably of dark complexion. They were of medium height, with skulls flattened by papoose boards, and in general with little to distinguish them from southern tribes. As regards their antiquity, and the length of time which they inhabited these cañons, all is shrouded in mystery. But I am inclined to think that the claim that I have made a few pages back, that the ruins or buildings may have

stood for a thousand years, allows sufficient time
for the period of building, occupying, and desertion
of these picturesque dwelling places. As for the
identity of race, in the absence of all reliable testimony I am content to accept the statement of
Wap, the Ute Indian, that they were the fore-
fathers of certain Pueblo tribes who now occupy
lands to the south,[1] regarding it as the more significant because, being uttered in a burst of indig-
nation, it was doubtless the expression of a deeply
grounded belief.

[1] See chapter x., the Ute Indians, p. 117.

CHAPTER XVI.

THE MESA VERDE.

THE Mesa Verde is the name [1] given to the high plateau which rises above the Mancos and Montezuma valleys to a height of from fifteen hundred to two thousand feet. Roughly speaking, it is about twenty by thirty miles in extent, and thus contains over six hundred square miles.

The surrounding country to the north and west has been eroded, leaving this plateau standing alone. It would seem, when observed from below, as if the top were nearly level; but this is far from the fact: the surface is undulating. Moreover, Mancos Cañon cuts through the entire length of the plateau, and as the side cañons head near the outer rims, the seeming solid mass is but a shell. The work of erosion is still going on, at least in winter, when volumes of water from the

[1] This plateau was named the "Mesa Verde" by Dr. J. S. Newberry when he, as geologist, accompanied the exploring expedition of Capt. J. N. Macomb. At that time its sides were covered with grass.

melting snows flow down the cañons and over the cliffs. The capping is of sandstone, and the greater part of the plateau is built up of layers of this same material, though this geological formation is interlaid with strata of friable nature which are more easily eroded, leaving the firmer rock standing as sheer precipitous walls. The top of the Mesa, except on the highest points, is covered with a scrubby forest of juniper and piñon trees Indian and game trails lead through this open forest in every direction.

There are several ways of ascending or descending with pack-mules and horses, — an important consideration, as a journey without pack-animals is out of the question; for blankets and provisions should be taken for a stay of several days. One route is to descend the main cañon of the Mancos to a point between Cliff and Navajo Cañons, where a good Indian trail leads to the plateau. It is not so steep nor so difficult as that leading to the opposite mesa. Another trail leads from Mancos Valley to Point Lookout. This is much travelled by cattle, and the paths are well worn. A third leads from the Montezuma Valley, and was never used except by Indians until we passed over it in September, 1890. It is not easy to find, especially in making the descent. Our party tried to get down the cliffs in many places before we discovered the true route. We wasted several hours, and descended in vain to considerable distances at different points of the Mesa's edge, and were as often obliged to climb up again. At last we found an encampment of Indians, of a party which had come from Ute Mountain, and descended by their trail.

The summit of the plateau is very dry, water being found in but few places. Occasionally it remains in "tanks" some time after a rainfall. These "tanks" are of special interest, from the fact that they were used by the Cliff-Dwellers. In some cases they were walled up to increase their capacity, and, where the sides were steep and slippery, steps were cut in the rock to enable the carriers to descend and bail out the water. Similar natural cisterns are also found in dry streams in the bed of the cañons. Once we searched long for such a place, riding till late in the night over an almost impassable trail; and we should have been obliged to camp without water if we had not discovered some cattle belonging to the Utes, which gave us the clew, following which we came to a tank.

On the Mesa, near the brink of Cliff Cañon, not far from the great ruin, is such a tank; but while camping there we gave it up to our animals, as there is a good spring in a short box-cañon near at hand, from which we could conveniently draw up the water over the cliff with lassos.

On another occasion we suffered from extreme thirst. Our canteens were empty, and we searched in vain for tanks on the Mesa. We separated, and followed the brink of cañons, looking below for pools. Search for ruins was given up; we were engrossed with our search for water. Finally one sighted it in a pool below, and answering his call, we gathered on the edge of the cañon. There, down in the depths, was a little round, yellow, dirty-looking puddle. It did not look inviting, but we knew it was good, for it was rainwater, and there were no signs of alkaline incrustations near it. We descended at break-neck speed, and spent an hour by its side.

It is difficult to find places of descent for horses and mules into the tributary cañons. The walls, except near the western rim of the plateau, are very abrupt, and when one rides along the Mesa, he frequently finds that he has arrived at a jumping-off place, for he is between two of the branches. The easiest places of descent are by the main cañous.

The Navajos have kept sheep and horses on the

Mesa, using for a corral the area between two box-cañons, which is cut off from the main plateau by a fence of juniper-trees.

There are many ruins on the Mesa, but they are so dilapidated that it is impossible to form an idea of their construction. A tower is yet standing between the forks of Navajo Cañon and another on the brink of one of the tributaries. This latter is a very picturesque sight when observed from the ravine below ; it commands a good view, and may have been used as a place of lookout. The places of burial were near the houses, and here it is that we find such an abundance of broken pottery, while a most fascinating variation is the search for arrow-heads. I found a number of very pretty specimens in an hour's time spent among some of these mounds. Similar ruins are found at the base of the Mesa, among the sand-hills of the northern side.

Let me finally describe one of our journeys across the Mesa. Our camp was on the brink of Cliff Cañon. We reached it long after dark ; and after the usual hard riding after stray horses, we got everything to rights, and whiled away the evening hours by a huge fire. Such a blaze as juniper and piñon pines make ! — a fire easy to build, and of lasting brilliancy.

The next morning dawned warm and bright, with a pleasant light breeze. We were up at sunrise, and off at eight o'clock, delaying only to photograph the camp and pack-animals. Our route lay to the north, along the mesa summit, and between Cliff and Navajo Cañons, which here run nearly parallel with the main one. We passed near the ends of many tributaries of these gorges, which showed that while it was a comparatively easy matter to get out of this country to the north, to come back to any given point from that direction would be impossible to any one not familiar with all the arms of the different cañons. Reversing the case of a mouse and a wire trap, it is easy enough to get out, but difficult to get in.

We observed no traces of ancient roads on the Mesa, nor of irrigating ditches; but we passed the ruins of what appears to have been a large reservoir.

At about ten o'clock we were at the heads of Navajo and Cliff Cañons; and soon we were so near the west end of the Mesa that we caught a glimpse of the broad Montezuma Valley. All the morning we followed trails leading through the extensive chaparral of juniper and piñon trees. The piñons were loaded with nuts, which are good eating. The Indians make flour from them, and subsist on it in certain seasons. Flying about were many piñon birds. The trails were made by Indians, deer, or cattle. We caught sight of three deer in the morning, and our dog brought a wild steer to bay, which threatened at one time to run us down.

About noon we reached the summit of the Mesa, at a point about an hour south of the promontory which marks the entrance to Mancos Cañon. A most remarkable view was unfolded. Over the pastoral scenes of the valley of Mancos, beyond the deep cañons of the Dolores River, far away in the north, loomed the snowy crests of the San Juan Mountains : Lone Cone, and the San Miguel on the left, then the Ouray group, with the grand peaks which we had climbed, flanked on the south by the mountains of Silverton and the Needles of the Rio de las Animas. Far away in the east rose range upon range which we could not identify with certainty. In the west were the Blue Mountains of Utah, Sierra Abajo, and Sierra la Sal. To the south and southwest stretched the great system of labyrinthine cañons, and far beyond were the Carisso Mountains of New Mexico. Here, within sight of our valley, and within a few hours' ride of it, we were able to while away the midday hours, and — as perhaps the former inhabitants of this strange land may have done at this same outlook — watch the panorama.

Resting on this summit, it was interesting to recall many incidents of our trip, and discuss the antiquities visited.

Looking over the wide stretch of country, we recalled the fact that to the early explorers this land seemed a desert. And well indeed it might. Over the wide arid plains stretch miles of waste acres covered with sage-brush and grease-wood. Yet all along the tops of the great Mesa over which we had been riding, pottery is strewn and signs of a primitive race are found. Its numbers must have been large, or the period of their stay prolonged.

It has been inferred by some writers that there must formerly have been a greater annual rainfall, in order that such a population could have been supported by agricultural employment; but judging from so much evidence that we found in the way of tanks and fragments of large water-jars, it would appear that the country was lacking in water even when occupied by the Cliff-Dwellers. And the hypothesis of a change of climate therefore becomes unnecessary. That the vanished race could have gained subsistence by tillage of the soil, seems evidenced by what the farmers of

Mancos and Montezuma Valleys are doing. This success shows what the lowlands, at least, are capable of producing, with irrigation. We find, however, no vestiges of ditches on the Mesa, and there is not much water to turn into such channels, if they did exist. Yet, on the tableland on which thrive such forests of juniper and piñon, enough grass grows to support much game and many cattle;. and the time may come when the land, grasped by the oncoming mightier race, will be overturned and tilled, and all along the broad tablelands and in many of the fertile cañon beds we shall see the tasselled maize bend, and fields of wheat wave to the breeze. Then it will no longer seem incredible when we read that the country once supported a great population, a people well advanced in many arts, and who conceived of certain forms of beauty, even though they lacked the ability to reproduce them in artistic shapes. And may we not imagine them a race who loved peace rather than war, but who, hard pressed by a savage foe, fought stubbornly and long, and died rather than desert their romantic fortresses among the cañon cliffs ?

INDEX.